The Good Gardener

Published by Linden Hills Press (a division of the Hohman Group, Inc.)

Trade distribution by Voyageur Press
P.O. Box 338
Stillwater, MN 55082

Page Layout and Assembly by Great Way Communications
Printed and bound in the United States by
Anderberg-Lund Printing Company

ISBN 0-9628378-0-6

Acknowledgements

The publisher is grateful to the following persons for making this book a reality. Dorothy Johnson for seeing the possibility. Jack Anderberg for his faith in us. Jodi Lind-Hohman of ARTGARDEN for her keen eye in selecting photos and for sharing her horticultural knowledge. The people at Great Way Communications for being able to follow my sometimes cryptic instructions. All the contributors to the Minnesota Horticulturist for their love of gardening and the ability and desire to share their many talents with the rest of us.

Thank you,
David Hohman
Publisher

Table of Contents

Chapter 1: Planning and Design

Chapter 2: Garden Basics

Chapter 3: Getting Started

Chapter 4: Care and Feeding

Chapter 5: Appendices

Foreword

The Northern Gardener's Library is based upon articles originally published in *Minnesota Horticulturist* magazine. Trusted as a reliable resource to northern horticulture for more than 100 years, *Minnesota Horticulturist* is the oldest continuously-published periodical in Minnesota. The official publication of the Minnesota State Horticultural Society, *Minnesota Horticulturist* began by relating experiences of horticulturists who moved to Minnesota to help feed the growing population. These pioneers faced unexpected challenges, attempting to grow the fruits and vegetables they brought from Europe and the Eastern United States.

Minnesota Horticulturist has evolved to meet the needs of amateur horticulturists — gardeners who enjoy their hobby within small or large home grounds. Writers share their own experiences, which bring research and experimentation to a practical level in the home garden.

This book shares the experience of seasoned gardeners, many of whom write regularly for *Minnesota Horticulturist*. Their practical advice is based upon observations, trials and successes. Care has been taken to explain environmentally-conscious techniques and growing practices.

The first two volumes in The Northern Gardener's Library are being published in 1991: *The Good Gardener* and *Flower Gardens*. Future volumes will feature other popular horticultural themes.

All of the volumes in the series concentrate on the unique needs and challenges of growing home gardens in the lovely, but often harsh, climates of the Upper Midwest. Written for hardiness zones 3 and 4, the information on culture and varieties is also valuable for zone 5 gardens.

Introduction

Good gardening begins with learning the basics: soil, water, nutrients, light and temperature are all important elements in plant growth. Additionally, in northern climates, the difference between success and failure often depends on timing and techniques

The Good Gardener is here to help! This book shares steps to productive results. Northern writers give realistic answers to how, when and why, as they review ideas for landscape planning, the basics of plant growth, and garden projects.

Does gardening begin in May? Not according to Fred Glasoe, who starts his catalog shopping as each year begins, and tends seedlings indoors during winter months. **How hardy is hardy?** John Masengarb helps us understand what grows in the North, and a map illustrates plant hardiness zones. **How should grass be cut?** Don Olson shares understandable, environmentally-conscious lawn care techniques.

Start with a landscape plan or a vegetable plot. *The Good Gardener* is a guide to success, with do-it-yourself tips on tree planting, herb and vegetable choices, and so much more. The book will also help readers make environmentally-sound choices which suit their lifestyles.

The northern gardeners who write for *Minnesota Horticulturist* are happy to share *The Good Gardener* with you.

Dorothy B. Johnson
Minnesota State Horticultural Society
Executive Director

Chapter 1

Planning and Design

Building a Better Garden

Thoughts on Landscape Design

Texture in the Home Landscape

Good Gardener's Design Checklist

Building a Better Garden

Fred Glasoe

If this were to be my first spring of gardening, I'd slow down the start. I'd take more time to develop a better soil base for all of my garden beds. Soil really is the biggest and most important item in any garden, whether it be a flower bed, a vegetable production area, or a nook of flowering shrubs.

Soil must have a spongy, organic base which encourages good drainage. It must be so loose that you can work your hand and arm down through it to the elbow. When you hold it in your hand and take a big sniff, it should have that lovely, woodsy, organic smell—reminiscent of well-decomposed leaf compost, old wood chips and sawdust, weeds from the lake, and well-rotted, organic barnyard residue.

Perhaps before I get that soil worked and conditioned, I would decide where and how I would grow my garden. I would want to take more time designing my garden, even if it meant doing only a little at a time. I certainly have learned not to attempt to do the whole thing in one year, and I know that some of my best-loved gardens have taken at least five years to develop. Over-gardening kills both the spirit and the spine. After many years of back-yard beautification, I wonder why I spent so many working hours on a garden that was seldom seen. We do not do enough front-yard gardening in the Midwest. We seem to be in love with that flat, grassy look of the prairie.

I would make my new garden graceful, with curling, interwoven borders. Bermed and raised outer beds would be set within brick paths that, in later years, would be green with moist algae. I would mix annuals and colorful, hardy perennials and include screens and frames of small evergreens and blooming shrubs. I would try to get away from the flat monotony of the common rectangular gardens that are always backed into a garage or fence.

Raised beds are a new garden innovation with many merits, particularly for the folks who inherit a poor soil base of hardpan or washed sand. By building raised beds 18 to 24 inches high, you can create or purchase the perfect garden soil for the plants you choose to grow. Soil is as important as air, water, or light conditions. The pH factor in the soil is perhaps more important than the addition of minerals, though we often test for lack of minerals in our growing areas. The pH of a soil is the measure of the amount of acid or alkali in the soil. The number seven on the scale is neutral. Going down the scale towards zero indicates the soil is more acidic. Acidic soils are not all bad. Actually, a pH of 6.5 to 6.8 will satisfy most common flowers or vegetables. There are a few alkali-loving species, and some plants such as rhododendrons, azaleas and hibiscus are acid-lovers.

Spring bulbs provide the first blooms to brighten our gardens. (Hodson)

I learned long ago to be careful about using too much lime in a garden. We get much of our water from deep, limestone aquifers that tend to neutralize acidic soils. There may be a few folks who live in high timber areas with many evergreens who would find the addition of lime an advantage. In any case, an electric pH meter is a very handy and inexpensive item for a serious gardener to own.

After thoughtfully dealing with soil and design, I would next make my plant choices. Selecting dependable varieties is very important. It has taken me years of trial and error to realize that pretty pictures and award winners are not always reliable indicators. Some plants are good, reliable growers, and others have continual problems. I like to watch what other gardeners are growing, and I like to visit their gardens several times during the season.

Flower gardens should burst forth with color at least four times a year. I have tried to create an early spring garden of spring bulbs, following these closely with early summer perennials. I use peonies—some singles and some Japanese hybrids. Along with these, I plant iris, Oriental poppies, coral bells, lupines, and campanulas of different varieties. Midsummer perennials follow, and these include lilies, daylilies, delphiniums, phlox, daisies, astilbe, heliopsis, monarda, cone flowers, rudbeckia, and many varieties of veronica. These provide more than quick, passing glimpses of color. After that, every garden should be filled with the fall beauty of chrysanthemums and dahlias. The bronzes, golds, yellows, and reds of these late garden giants blend well with the turning colors of the trees and shrubs. White chrysanthemums, which would never stand out in the summer, are simply outstanding against the deeply colored background of a fall landscape. It's fun to plan for that major crescendo of color before everything disappears, succumbing to winter's bleakness.

Perennials are the backbone of the flower garden, but in order to maintain a full season of bloom, we must use some constantly blooming, faithful annuals. These one-season plants should be used in masses of a single color. It's the best technique for creating intensity in those areas among and between the perennials. You can achieve "double color" with deeply planted tulips, which give way to a single variety of annuals planted above the bulbs. Surprising color splashes will surface in the open ovals situated between the old reliables which come back every year.

It's far better to plant only a few varieties in large amounts, closely compacted, than to grab a push cart at the local nursery and fill it

Nicotiana is a popular annual whose fragrant blooms are a favorite of Hummingbirds. (Shannon)

with too many one-of-a-kind small boxes. A few plants will not be noticed in any garden. The onlooker shouldn't have to strain to see color. A snapdragon here and a snapdragon there makes for no sight of snapdragons anywhere. Colorful annuals such as impatiens, petunias, geraniums, nicotiana, zinnias, marigolds, snapdragons, salvia, celosia, and my favorite, fibrous begonias, should be planted in large amounts and close together for a big flash of color from mid-June until frost.

I like to fill my beds and borders with mass plantings of bright geraniums. In order to show them off in true and best form, you need dozens. It used to mean a lot of money spent on potted greenhouse plants, but now folks can explore the fun of growing geraniums under fluorescent lights. With a minimum investment in fixtures, I can grow about 200 geraniums, seeding them January 1 while I listen to the football bowl games. For about eight dollars per 100 seeds, the price is right.

Too many gardeners worry about sprays and powders. Healthy plants, in good, light, always-moist soil are not very vulnerable to insects and fungi. If a spray is needed, a systemic insect spray once or twice a month sometimes spreads less harmful poisons than weaker sprays used once a week.

It's easy to overfeed plants.

The large flower clusters of the geranium are highlighted in contrast to the silver foliage of the border planting 'Dusty Miller'. (C. King)

Unless you are growing leafy crops such as cabbage or lettuce, or ornamental hostas or coleus, large amounts of nitrogen can prevent blooming or fruiting. Fertilize those open annual and bulb areas after clearing out the old debris in October. A general balanced fertilizer with all the numbers the same, such as 10-10-10, is fine. The number order stands for 10 percent nitrogen, 10 percent phosphate, and 10 percent potassium. If you want to stimulate a plant to grow strong roots and stems and to flower freely, drop the percentage of nitrogen and increase the second and third numbers. Vegetable gardeners should be especially careful in purchasing and using fertilizers to promote and force the growth of the edible parts of plants. Annuals need less fertilizer than perennials and will bloom much more freely in what gardeners call poor, light soil. Clay holds nutrients for a long period of time, while sandy soils are leached out in two or three rainfalls or in just a few weeks of watering in hot weather.

Remember that we don't give every plant the same fertilizer. Check your soil, decide which plant parts need accentuation of growth, and make an estimate of how much watering should be done each week. Water, of course, is really a food for plants. Fluids containing plant sugars are results of water, carbon dioxide, and sunlight. Soil that holds moisture and air at the same time will grow good plants. Other than an automatic watering system, the best thing I have found is a black sweat hose. An overnight soaking for six or eight hours once a week keeps the soil moist yet not flooded, and the water doesn't remain on foliage as an invitation to fungus invasion. Always moist, yet never wet, is a good maxim for successful outdoor gardens. Keeping the garden dressed with a mulch of chopped leaves provides adequate moisture retention, even on very hot days.

Serious green thumbers, as some folks have labelled us, love to grow one or two hobby plants. These are usually perennials, grown in their own special areas or beds. Among the most popular are roses, dahlias, peonies, irises, lilies, hostas, daylilies, and of course, the retiree's favorite—gigantic tomatoes. Each of these plants become like personal friends or children. They have their own varietal names, their own colors and shapes, and their special challenges. Clubs and societies exist which produce special shows each year to promote the exchange of information. Growers meet to spend an hour of "how to" information and to study the new hybrids. It's fun to be involved in these specialized plant societies because as you read, study, and

Plantings of early summer perennials, such as iris, provide a continuation of color from the blooms of spring bulbs. (MSHS)

talk about your specialties, you can develop into something of an expert. Hobby plants are fun to grow and often provide unusual size, color, and exceptional beauty. It's not difficult, and you can find tons of informational material and friends to help you along the way.

I particularly like to grow roses because I get the most bloom for the longest time with the least amount of work. They provide a constantly changing, satisfying garden scene. I have succeeded because I met very fine rose growers who were more than willing to help me at the start. I still get together with these folks. We enjoy both our flowers and the friends they have helped us make.

Gardening is fun and relaxing if it is done over a long period of time without the goal of instant success. Trial and error provide the best learning experiences. As the garden fades in late fall, I start to wait impatiently for next spring, filling my winter mind with new ideas. I recall the gardens I have visited, the talks with friends about gardening methods, each one with its own special merits. The garden grows year by year. As I slowly expand its boundaries, my love for the world of plants and for my gardening friends grows. It seems to me that my adventures in my ever-changing, improving garden are some of my greatest delights.

Thoughts on Landscape Design

Jon Bryan Burley

Over the past several decades, writers on landscape design have perpetuated many design guidelines that have outlived their usefulness. Some of these principles are outdated, while others are misconceptions. Here are some suggestions of which rules to follow — and which to break— in redesigning and improving the landscapes of the future.

Misconception #1 concerns the notion that each plant must have its own space and be separated from each and every other plant. While it is true that plants do require space to grow, individual plants are not always desirable. Separate plants bring attention to themselves. Unless the individual plants are the most important feature of the landscape, it is preferable to create a mass planting which emphasizes the use of a particular space.

Arboretums and botanical gardens are examples of places where individually placed plants are desirable so the plants can be examined and studied as specimens. Unfortunately, when the public visits these gardens they some- times gain the impression that their personal residential garden should look like an arboretum.

Before preparing a planting design, identify the purpose of the planting; plant locations should reflect purpose. Screening, privacy, noise or erosion control, wind buffering, wildlife planting, microclimate modification, shading, energy efficiency, mass color, and fragrance — all are examples of planting for a purpose. Plants are placed in proximity to one another and the result is an image where one plant's space is indistinguishable from the next plant's space.

Misconception #2 is that colorful plants, colorful mulches, and carefully trimmed plants must be used everywhere throughout the landscape. While it is true that color and clean, crisp shapes can make a dull space more lively, pervasive color and rigidity often produce chaotic spaces. Homeowners and some designers are tempted to use an abundance of purple, golden, variegated, and red-colored foliage plants in the landscape, clip every reachable plant into round balls, or place colorful planting islands into the middle of large open lawns. This approach is analogous to wearing a yellow shirt with a red sportcoat, lime green pants, white shoes, and a plaid tie. Such an assortment of colors and rigid shapes often becomes tiring and hard on the eyes. Landscapes with abundant loud colors should be left to amusement parks.

In most commercial and residential landscapes, the use of colorful plants and formal shapes should be limited to points of emphasis, such as entryways and signage. Usually the colorful plants should be used with discretion, restraint, and only in concert with the general concept. Avoid meaningless islands of flowers. Place flowers next to entryways, patios, and decks.

Carefully pruned plants and plants with unusual shapes should also be used exclusively at points of importance. Plants should be coordinated to emphasize clearly (or de-emphasize) the importance of each space. In residential landscapes there may be only one or two special areas requiring emphasis, such as the patio or front entryway.

Misconception #3 assumes that certain elements in the landscape must be hidden, softened, or diligently defined. Foundation plantings are an example, using plants to skirt around a structure and supposedly hide the building's foundation. This technique is also used in covering utility boxes and meters, dog pens, and air conditioners. By using plants to screen or cover unsightly features, the homeowner or designer often brings unmerited attention to the very things they mean to conceal.

Border planting is another example where designers and homeowners carefully delineate the property line, as though the land must be defended. Instead, play upon the positive aspects of the structure or landscape, and ignore those aspects which make little difference in creating an exciting, livable landscape.

The planned landscape should consider the style of architecture, land forms, circulation patterns, or ecology and concentrate upon articulating the space to extend these elements into the landscape. If you have a very rectilinear house, you might concentrate upon rectangles and 90-degree angles in designing the landscape. If, on the other hand, it's a lake home nestled in woodlands, you might concentrate on the natural shapes and patterns of the surrounding landscape.

Inspiration for design should ideally come from the characteristics of the site, rather than from antiquated rules concerning foundation plantings and border plantings. Each landscape has the potential to be special. Residential landscapes which contain the same few identical species and spatial arrangements are boring and unimaginative.

Misconception #4 concerns the actual selection of plant species. Problems arise from designs that contain 20 to 30 plant species in a small area, or contain plants with borderline hardiness, or plants that grow too large or remain too small.

Typically, planting many species in a small area draws unwarranted attention to that specific area. Designs with many species appear to be plant collections. Numerous plant species tend to slice the landscape into fragments. Planting too many species is like creating a structure with too many design materials. Rarely does one see a building containing plaster, brick, stucco, aluminum siding, tinted glass, stainless steel, wood siding, and flagstone. Yet many people insist upon creating a landscape with a large collection of unrelated plants. Instead, the designer should try to unify the space through restraining the number of plant species. Many residential landscapes can be adequately designed with only five or six plant species.

Often people select vegetation which is not hardy or is ill-adapted to the particular growing conditions of the site. Hardiness, soil pH, moisture abundance, sunlight, and degree of physical disturbance are environmental characteristics that need to be considered when choosing plant material. Take the time to learn about the needs of the plants you like and match your plant materials with your environment.

Abuses regarding size often occur when selecting plant material. Many attractive little plants, which will eventually become large trees, are placed under eaves or utility wires. Learn to allow for the future size of your plants, not just their present space requirements

Misconception #5 thinks of the landscape as a two-dimensional form. While framing or creating a specific view serves to add depth and interest from a specific point, most landscapes are experienced from a series of points. As a person moves through the landscape, there should be a series of enclosures and openings revealing entrances and user activities. Framing one view from one specific point can lead to a monotonous landscape. Landscapes should be treated by carefully examining the total landscape during all seasons and during the life expectancy of that landscape.

Misconception #6 concerns the overabundance of grass and lawns in most northern landscapes.. The rule of thumb is "when in doubt, plant turf grasses." Yet lawns requires extensive maintenance. Grasses are a specialized plant material, suitable for receiving a marginal amount of foot traffic. In areas where foot traffic is not a problem, naturalized landscapes should be implemented.

Presently, there is a movement toward naturalized lawns. The city of Madison, Wisconsin, has a naturalized lawn ordinance which allows the creation of non-bluegrass areas. The city of Moorhead, Minnesota, developed a similar ordinance. Riverbank landscapes, lakeshore lots, woodland lots, and prairie landscapes are potential sites where naturalized lawns may be more appropriate.

Seeds for Thought

Remember that there are no hard and fast rules concerning landscape design. Here are a few general recommendations, however, that should help you develop a better landscape design.

- A landscape should have an identifiable, but discrete, purpose. Make spaces for people.

- Use plants to refine and emphasize the purpose of the space.

- Rely upon some intrinsic characteristic of the site or of the homeowner as inspiration for design. Do not mindlessly copy traditional designs.

- Spend some time studying the environmental characteristics of the site and select plants which match these environmental characteristics. Restrict the planting palette to a limited number of species.

- Consider the site from all sides, not just from one view. Create space for people to walk through and experience, throughout the seasons and from year to year.

- Avoid using lawn where it is not required.

Texture in the Home Landscape

Emely Lincowski

A large part of the alluring charm of many attractive gardens can be attributed to texture, the frequently forgotten element of landscape design. Don't miss a chance to consciously incorporate texture, when planning and designing your home landscape.

To the designer, texture is one of three elements of design to be considered when planning a landscape; the other two are form and color. These three elements interact in a design to produce the desired visual landscape effect. Whether in a formal garden, the urban spaces of city parks and avenues, or a home landscape, texture is important in forming the character of that space.

Texture is defined as the surface appearance of an object. It can be described as soft, hard, smooth, rough, fine or large. However, texture is not simply appearance, but the appearance of the smallest part in relation to the total size of the object. Picture a stone wall. It may appear very rough when made of stones four inches in diameter, if the wall is only one foot in height. The same sized stone, in a much taller wall, can give the appearance of a smooth finish.

Another factor which affects our perception of texture is the distance from which the object or space is viewed. The stone wall concept applies here, too — at close range the wall appears rough; from a distance, the same wall may appear smooth.

Two general sources of texture appear in the landscape, natural materials and man-made materials. Natural materials include plants and other naturally occurring elements, such as rocky outcroppings, ponds or lakes, and rivers. Architectural or man-made materials include buildings, walls, fences, walks, and paved areas.

Architectural materials vary greatly in their textural appearance: concrete seems smooth and cold; brick is considered warm in color and good for adding texture through its versatility of patterns; stone can be smooth or rough depending on the type and cut; wood is highly versatile in providing texture through its cut, pattern, and finish.

The natural materials, on the

other hand, have more subtle textural qualities which are heightened when viewed at close range. The conscious application of texture in the landscape involves the use of these subtleties played against each other and against the texture of the architectural materials. Contrasts in texture, and the proportion of natural to architectural elements, influence our perception of a space.

Plant materials are frequently used to "soften" or remove the hardness imparted by concrete, stone and brick. The addition of any greenery, without much thought to its inherent texture, will immediately bring necessary relief to built spaces. Generally, the greater the ratio of plant materials to architectural materials, the less rigid the space will appear; it will seem more welcoming and relaxing.

A concrete patio adjacent to a home will require careful planning to make it an appealing, usable area. Selecting plants to create softness and applying them in proper scale and proportion will determine the desired mood of the patio, from secluded and intimate to open and less private. On the other hand, areas incorporating brick, stone, and wood seem to have a degree of inherent charm and texture, and need only to be liberated by discrete selection and placement of plants.

Imaginative use of natural materials gives this small English courtyard garden a warm, inviting feel. (J. Hohman)

The gardens of England contain many noteworthy examples of texture in the landscape. There, liberal use of stone and brick for building and paving set the groundwork for strong textural interest. The wide diversity of available plant material further enhances the richness of the designs.

In the northern United States, the palette of available plants is reduced, but the same effects can be created. When designing your space, consider its function. Will it be viewed from the distance or is it an area to be viewed at close proximity? Landscape areas to be viewed from afar benefit from bold-textured plants and a more daring use of contrast. Here are a number of suggestions:

Ornamental grasses add a sense of drama to the northern garden. (C. King)

- Large-leaved plants of coarser texture — such as hosta, canna, alchemilla, bergenia, and ligularia — can be used in greater doses when viewed from a distance. Contrast them with the more delicate-textured perennials, shrubs, and evergreens.

- Ornamental grasses — such as reed grass, fountain grass, phalaris and Chinese pennisetum — provide drama and are a wonderful contrast to the bold-textured plants.

- Evergreens provide a variety of surface appearances: the fluffy cloud look of mugo pines, roundish fans of arborvitae, spikes of juniper, and the thread-like foliage of Sawara false cypress.

- Attractive groupings are produced by using reed grass, creeping junipers, and dwarf fir.

- Another interesting selection of plants for grouping are *Sedum spectabile,* Chinese pennisetum and mugo pine.

Entryway, patio, and deck areas require a smaller, more intimate scale. Fine-textured plants and more subtle contrasts produce interesting effects that would be lost if viewed from afar. This is not to say that bold-textured plants are not used in these areas, but they are used as accents, where greater contrast is needed, or to focus attention on a particular spot.

- Herbs are a favorite for adding textural interest; many have fine textures and are a manageable size for small quarters. They have the added benefit of providing fragrance if touched or crushed. Thyme offers a delicate texture and is very attractive for planting between stone paving or amidst rockery. Woolly thyme, as the name implies, is covered with a layer of woolly hairs that impart a bluish cast to the foliage. Catmint 'Blue Wonder' is a substitute for the effect provided by lavender in warmer climates.

- Lambs-ears have white, woolly, hairy foliage that appears to have a silvery sheen. It makes a good companion to plants with finer texture such as veronica 'Red Fox'.

- Flowers also have their own textural qualities. Veronica 'Red Fox', salvia 'East Friesland', limonium, and gypsophila have fine-textured, yet showy, flowers.

Cascades of yellow dramatically soften this set of garden steps and makes them even more informal. (MSHS)

The Good Gardener's Design Checklist
by Dorothy Johnson

GOAL: A GARDEN TO FIT MY LIFESTYLE

☐ What are my priorities for my yard?

☐ How much time can I spend on care *and* enjoyment?

☐ Do changes in family composition change expectations for my yard and garden?

☐ Should I consider major renovation, change of location or different plant mixture?

☐ Is gardening my passion or an incidental hobby?

GOAL: DEFINE THE GARDEN AS A SEPARATE SPACE WITHIN THE YARD

☐ Have I assessed and planned the uses of the entire yard?

☐ Does the garden have an enclosed feeling, with plants or structures for background?

☐ Does it invite visitors to explore at close range?

☐ Is there a seating area to rest and enjoy plants?

GOAL: PLEASING VIEWS IN EVERY SEASON

☐ How does my garden look from inside, especially from windows where family and visitors usually view the yard?

☐ Do I consider views onto adjacent properties?

☐ Where does the garden look best for outdoor viewing?

☐ Do I keep records of bloom times and other plant features?

☐ Are color combinations pleasant to my eye?

☐ Are colors planned in masses, not dots?

☐ Is there constant color during the growing season?

☐ Do evergreens enhance my winter vistas?

☐ Have I studied size, shape, foliage and growth habit of plants I intend to add to the garden?

GOAL: EXCELLENT PLANT PERFORMANCE

☐ Have I reviewed the garden basics at my site (soil type, sunlight, drainage, winds, microclimate)?

☐ Do I know what plants grow best in these conditions?

☐ Has growth or loss of trees impacted growing conditions?

☐ Are current plantings the most hardy varieties available?

☐ Are new varieties available which bloom longer or more dependably than current plantings?

☐ Am I learning the best options in northern gardening by reading and attending seminars?

GOAL: REDUCE MAINTENANCE

☐ Do I consider maintenance requirements when choosing plants?

☐ Am I using mulch to keep soil cool, conserve moisture and hamper weed growth?

☐ Do I have a maintenance plan for watering, fertilizing, pruning and other basics?

☐ Have I considered drip irrigation for watering?

☐ When planting, do I add enough soil amendments to maintain healthy, long-term plant growth?

☐ Would paths, edging, raised beds or terracing make gardening easier and more enjoyable?

Chapter 2

Garden Basics

Ingredients for Great Gardens

Composting Basics

Understanding Plant Hardiness

Ingredients For Great Gardens

Fred Glasoe

Watering

Water keeps plants growing by allowing roots to take up food. Soil that has been well prepared and mulched will need little watering except during dry spells. Don't wait until plants are severely wilted to water. Putting them under such stress causes them to sulk at the expense of bloom.

Water thoroughly. When dry, water once a week and apply one inch of water at a time. Frequent light watering encourages roots to grow near the soil surface, making the plant more susceptible to drought. The best way to water is with a soil soaker or a bubbler. With these methods there is very little evaporation or run-off, and the water seeps deep into the soil. Deep watering encourages deep rooting, and plants with well-formed root systems can withstand dry periods better. Remember also that the type of plant will determine the need for water. Shallow-rooted plants will need more frequent watering than deep-rooted plants.

If using overhead watering, water early in the day so that the foliage will dry quickly. Foliage that goes into the evening wet is especially vulnerable to fungus diseases, such as mildew.

Fertilizer

Fertilizer contains the elements which promote growth in our plants. It's important to know which plant parts these minerals support. Most garden fertilizers consist of 30 to 40 percent useable elements and 60 to 70 percent neutral filler. The working elements in fertilizers are nitrogen, phosphorous, and potassium. These are indicated by the percentage number on the container, such as 20-10-10. Some secondary elements such as iron, magnesium, calcium, sulphur, copper, zinc, or boron are often included.

Nitrogen, the first number in the analysis, keeps plants green and stimulates the growth of foliage. It is an excellent soil addition for such vegetables as lettuce, cabbage, chard, kale, and spinach. Dark green lawns and shade trees benefit greatly from high-nitrogen fertilizers. Both indoor and outdoor foliage plants find nitrogen a treat.

Look for a high second number if color or fruit production is what you desire. It indicates the phosphorous percentage. Phosphorous also stimulates root growth in new plants and root crops.

Potassium, represented by the third number, joins together as a catalyst with phosphorous, to ensure good metabolism, transpiration, and respiration in the plant. It also helps ensure hardiness and disease resistance.

We hear so much about organic and inorganic fertilizers. Both contain the elements that the plant world needs, but these elements are present in very different amounts and forms. Organic fertil-izers come from plant and animal tissue and waste. They are slow acting and not always balanced in the way in which they meet nutritional needs. They seldom burn stems and roots if they are directly applied, and they are good for soil building and conditioning.

Inorganic fertilizers are mined minerals or laboratory chemical compounds that are water soluble. The nutrients are released quickly and can damage plants if the fertilizer is not properly diluted. Although they are fast acting and efficient, they do nothing to build up a good bulky, aerated soil, and should be used as a supplement to a good soil composting program.

Improving this tightly packed, hard clay soil requires the addition of organic matter such as compost. (MSHS)

Soil

Good garden soil should feel loose and crumble easily when squeezed. Most garden plants will not survive in poorly drained soil, such as the heavy clay-type soils which predominate in parts of the northern states. (Clay soil is easily identified. When wet, a handful of soil will hold together and feel sticky when squeezed. When dry, clay soils tend to become hard and cracked.) In some places, sandy soil prevails. (Sand cannot hold moisture, and nutrients are washed away from plant roots with constant watering.) Both clay and sandy soils need additions to become desirable growing media.

Seedlings get off to a fast start in rich, loose soil. (MSHS)

Sand added to clay or clay added to sand can improve overall soil composition. But the desired loam soil also contains organic matter. Compost, peat moss, decomposed farmyard manure, leaf mold, and grass clippings are the most important soil amendments for any soil type. Such organic matter will not only improve soil drainage, but will also promote aeration, reduce erosion, and supply plants with nutrients and micro-organisms which might otherwise be unavailable for plant use. Organic materials will also help to improve the general physical condition of the soil and aid in warming up the soil early in the spring.

To add organic materials, simply spread a two to three-inch layer over the surface of the garden. Thoroughly mix this layer into the existing soil by spading or roto-tilling. Barnyard manure should be well composted (not fresh) to avoid introducing weed seeds.

Mulching

Mulches provide surface insulation to help conserve moisture, modify soil temperature, and provide weed control. Apply mulch in late June, after soil is thoroughly warmed.

In the vegetable garden, mulches (such as straw, hay, leaf-mold, grass clippings, aged manure or aged sawdust) may be used. Flower gardens enjoy oak leaf mulch. Their addition will aid water absorption and water holding ability.

Organic additives worked into the soil prevent compaction and greatly improve aeration. Mulches and other organic additives are not fertilizers; if they are not completely broken down when they are worked into the soil, they will tie up soil nitrogen during their breakdown. This may result in poor plant growth and the need for additional nitrogen fertilizer.

Before applying the mulch, water well; be sure that any crust on the soil surface has been broken and all weeds have been hoed out; then, it may be wise to apply a top dressing of a good garden grade fertilizer (10-10-10).

The mulch should be applied two or four inches deep, but do not pile mulch high around the plant stem. To do so would soften the stem and promote disease organisms. Keep the mulch low at the plant base, but mound it deep between the plants.

These are the ingredients for great gardens: adequate water, healthy soil, the right fertilizer mix, and a cooling mulch. Then add some regular attention and the result will be a healthy, bountiful, and beautiful garden.

Take advantage of the early-spring sun and warm the soil by placing black plastic over the soil. (MSHS)

Seeds for Thought

Spring
- Black plastic laid over freshly tilled soil will warm the soil and give plants a good start. Cut a hole for each plant, leaving space to water. In July, cover plastic with compost or grass clippings.
- Gardeners should resist the temptation to work the soil too early in spring, when the soil is often wet. Working wet soil can compact it, pushing out valuable air pockets and creating large soil clumps. Not only is aeration reduced, but the soil can become hard and cement-like. To tell if the soil is ready to be worked, take a handful and squeeze it. If the soil becomes a wet ball of mud the soil is obviously too wet and may need organic matter added to it. The soil is ready to work when the soil ball breaks up easily after squeezing it.

Summer
- Feeding both vegetables and flowers is important at this time of year. Overfeeding is just as bad as not feeding at all. If you want leaves, feed the plants a lot of nitrogen. If it's blooms you want, it might be best to skimp on nitrogen. Stems and roots need potash and phosphate for strong development. Both of these, especially the phosphate, will help flowers to form and bloom. Adequate nitrogen improves the quality of your foliage, but if your soil is heavy, keep in mind that a small amount will last a long time. Many new gardeners overfeed their annuals and have more leaves than flowers.
- If your flower garden has extremely healthy looking plants producing only a few flowers, check your fertilizer mix. Many gardeners automatically use a 10-10-10 food formula. Some should be using a 5-20-20 formula or even a 9-45-30. A soil test is definitely in order. Check with your local county Extension Service.

Fall
- Allow the surface of the turned-over garden to remain rough to achieve maximum benefit from the freeze-thaw cycle.
- Hold off applying all winter cover until the ground has received a permanent hard crust. Beginning gardeners often labor under the assumption that the main purpose of winter cover is to keep the plants warm. In reality, winter cover is used to stabilize the soil temperature, to prevent violent fluctuations in temperature. It is far better to cover late than too early.

Composting Basics

Beth Jarvis

Why Compost?

I'll admit that composting can be a bit of work. It takes me about one-half hour per week per pile to maintain them — but I think the time and effort is worth it. The first year I had a garden at our current home, I used compost from a municipal site. It worked fine, but I didn't care for the pieces of glass, wire, and plastic I kept finding. Making my own compost is good exercise, and it allows me to sort out life's problems while I work; it's a means of improving the soil at virtually no cost; it eliminates the need to buy soil enhancers; using compost as mulch cuts down on my water bill. Finally, I'm contributing, albeit in a small way, to the solution of one of the environment's most critical problems by reducing and recycling solid waste.

What Exactly is Compost?

I think of compost as a mixture of "greens" and "browns." The greens are the nitrogen-rich materials, like grass clippings, that add nutrients and help break down the other ingredients in the pile. The browns are organic materials, like dried leaves or sawdust. Add soil and water and what do you have? Compost!

Building a Compost Bin

Before you can begin composting, you will need a way to contain your pile. One easy solution is to use 55 gallon drums with holes punched in them, providing air circulation. Make sure the drums have lids that fasten, so you can turn the compost heap by simply tipping the barrel over and rolling it on a weekly basis.

You can also make a very simple compost bin out of four pallets. Set three on edge at 90-degree angles to each other to make an open-ended, topless and bottomless box. The fourth pallet can be used as a door. You may wish to sink some metal posts in the ground to keep the three sides upright. One of the advantages of this loosely-constructed bin is its portability. To turn the pile, you can either move the compost or move the box — either shovel the compost out and pitch it back in; or take the sides down, set them up facing the old site, and pitchfork the compost into the newly-formed box.

The traditional compost bin is made from wood and wire mesh. Plans are available from a variety of sources. I used wood to frame a rectangular box eight feet long, four feet high, and four feet wide. There is a divider in the middle, which gives me two side-by-side bins. I enclosed it with wire mesh. I built it one Saturday and ended up with a respectable-looking structure, even though I had never done any woodworking before.

Compost piles work best if they are three to four feet wide. If they are smaller, the material will not break down as quickly. Anything larger becomes difficult to handle.

How to Compost

To start a pile, I lay about four inches of leaves on the ground as my base. Then I sprinkle about two inches of grass clippings over the leaves. I add another layer of leaves, more grass, and keep alternating layers until I'm out of grass clippings. I haven't found it necessary to add nitrogen to the pile, although some people sprinkle granulated garden fertilizer on every leaf layer, especially if they're short on clippings. Garden catalogs are anxious to sell something called compost starter — here again, I haven't found this necessary. Just adding soil works as well

and is much cheaper.

Dry material such as leaves, dead plant material from flower beds, along with the dead grass you rake up off your lawn in the spring provide the decomposed organic materials for the pile. Lumber yards and woodworking shops produce vast quantities of sawdust and wood shavings that can also be used and are generally free for the asking, if you bring your own bags. The larger the wood shaving, the longer it will take to break down. I've never tried just sawdust and grass but I have successfully used sawdust in a mix of grass and leaves. Old hay and straw can also be used.

When I build a new pile, I make a depression in the top of the heap to catch rainwater; I rarely need to add additional water. Much of the how-to literature suggests that you water every layer as you hide it, but in my experience, that makes the pile much too wet. In a normal spring, I get adequate moisture from the grass clippings and rain and do not need to water my compost heap. If it turns very dry, I set a slow-running hose on top of the heap and leave it there until water appears at the bottom of the pile. A weekly watering in this manner is plenty.

Maintaining the Pile

Once the pile is built, I let it sit for three to seven days; if the weather is hot I turn it in three days, otherwise it can sit a week. You don't have to turn it at all, but the more it is turned, the faster the materials will break down into usable compost. An unturned pile will take up to a year to break down. With weekly turnings, I can get usable compost in six to eight weeks.

The proper amount of moisture is an important factor in composting and a good part of the reason straight grass clippings will smell; they can retain too much moisture. If there is a lot of rain and the pile seems too wet, I spread out grass clippings in a low, wide heap in my back yard to let them dry a bit before adding them. As they dry, I turn them with a rake.

Decomposing plant material gives off heat as it breaks down. I can tell if my compost pile is working by checking to see if it heats up. If I put my hand into the new compost heap, I should feel heat within a foot of the surface. On cool spring mornings, my compost pile steams as I shovel it out. As I dig into the pile, I find parts of it are grey, as if burned to ash. The piles cease to heat up as the organic matter becomes more fully decomposed. A pile that is done will not heat up much at all.

If an active pile is not heating up, it is either too wet or short of nitrogen-rich materials like grass clippings; add grass clippings if the pile is not too wet, and it's still not heating. Alfalfa pellets are a good source of nitrogen, too. They're available at farm stores or in some types of cat litter.

When the first pile has started to break down nicely, I start a second pile in the other bin. This bin becomes the depository for all garden waste and grass clippings. I keep adding to this one until the first one is ready to be used. Then I clean out the first bin and use it on my flower and vegetable beds. I store the finished compost in a plastic garbage can and any other containers I can find to hold it. I start a new heap in the first bed and let the second one rest. Well, rest isn't exactly the right word. Each pile gets turned once a week, whether I add material to it or not. The purpose of turning the pile is to move the stuff on top down into the pile so it will rot and to aerate the pile.

Every Saturday morning while my husband is mowing our grass, I take my trusty garden fork and pitch the contents of the newest compost bin out. As he brings me clippings, I mix them into the compost heap and fork the compost back into the bin. (By this time the layer business is impossible to maintain.) The first time I turn a new heap, it's a bit unwieldy. It gets easier to handle as the material breaks down. I use a leaf rake to tidy the area and capture any errant leaves and grass I can't get with the fork.

Added Ingredients

What else do I put in my compost pile besides leaves and grass? I put in all garden waste, unless the plants are obviously diseased, like corn ears that have developed smut or squash vines infected with vine borers. I bury my tomato stalks at the base of a new pile in the hopes that the high temperatures will kill off any disease residues. I add peelings from carrots and potatoes, carrot tops and their like, overripe fruits or vegetables. I put weeds into a new pile, some with seed heads, and I count on the high temperatures of the compost heap to kill the weed seeds. I do not put in any meat, bones, or animal fats or by-prod-

ucts; these attract rodents. Nor will I put in any used cat litter or animal waste.

I turn the piles weekly and have not experienced any problem with mice. Spoiled matter, such as fruit, is covered with leaves to prevent flies from being attracted to the pile.

A compost pile will compress over time. You will not get a bag of compost for every bag of leaves and grass you put in. My experience tells me that the ratio is about four to one. In the fall I keep my compost bins full to the top — that's 64 cubic feet of organic material per bin. The pile shrinks about 25 percent per week. So, if the bin was full to the top one week, it will only be three-fourths full the second week. If I did not add more organic matter, I'd end up with about a quarter of the total volume when the compost was done.

Seeds for Thought

- If you have partially rotted compost which is thawed out by mid-April, you can sprinkle it liberally with nitrogen (urea) and turn it. To start the decomposition as soon as possible, be sure you have turned it over so that it is loose and well ventilated. The compost can be ready for your late garden planting in May if you can get it to generate enough heat.

Understanding Plant Hardiness

John Masengarb

Some winters, more than others, test the cold-hardiness of our garden perennials and woody landscape plants. In the spring we may notice that some of our trees, shrubs, and vines were killed back — at least to the point where the snow covered them. Winters such as these point out the importance of plant hardiness.

Why one kind of plant is hardier than another is a matter of genetics. What is important for us to know is not the why, but the degree of hardiness. In more ways than one, hardiness is a matter of degrees. Will the shrub we see, so nicely pictured in the catalog, still be alive and well in our front yard after a northern winter? Will the ground cover that grows so well for our relatives in Ohio grow here, too? This is what we want to know before we add it to our home landscape.

How can catalogs tell us how hardy their offerings are? How can your relatives give you an idea about whether or not their ground cover would survive here? There are only a few ways. One, they can tell you where it has survived.

("Has been growing in Yankton for 20 years.") Two, they can tell you the coldest temperature it has survived. ("Survived -12°F one winter.") Or three, they can do both at once, by telling you the plant's cold-hardiness zone rating. ("This shrub is suitable to Zone 3.")

A new USDA map was published in 1990, based on thousands of separate observations made in the last few years. It is believed to be both more accurate and current than any of its predecessors. The southern third of Minnesota is in Zone 4 (-30°F to -20°F), most of the central and northern portions are Zone 3 (-40°F to -30°F), with a couple of small islands of Zone 2 (-50°F to -40°F).

While cold hardiness ratings have, overall, been useful to American horticulture, there are several misconceptions that some of us have had about them. One is the idea that if a certain species is rated hardy for a certain zone, then any individual of that species should be able to survive in that zone. Take the example of red maple (*Acer rubrum*). Its native range extends from southern

Even in the colder climates, gardeners have an abundance of hardy plant varieties to work with in creating a memorable scene. (MSHS)

Manitoba, east to New Brunswick, south to central Florida, and west to east Texas. Not all of those red maples are the same. The ones in Florida are adapted to their area. They fail to harden off properly when brought further north. But then this brings us back to where we started — is it hardy, or isn't it?

Another related misconception is the idea that if a plant is rated for a zone, then it should be able to survive anywhere in that zone. A broad-leaved evergreen such as rose bay rhododendron doesn't prove as hardy in the dry, prairie portions of its zone as it does in the more humid, coastal areas of that zone. Remember, the zone maps are based only on average annual

low temperatures, and many other factors (rainfall, humidity, snow cover, even soil type) determine plant survival.

Another misconception is the idea that the zone is a solid band as it appears on the map, where minimum temperatures can be anywhere from -35°F to -20°F. Rather it is a range bounded by those two temperatures, and the southern portion will usually afford a higher hardiness rating than the northern edge.

Another misconception is that zone ratings are just another characteristic of plants. In other words, that there are "Zone 3 plants" or "Zone 4 plants." Sometimes a plant's zone is changed when more becomes known about its hardiness, or a new hybrid will be more cold-hardy than its parent plants.

So we shouldn't really find it remarkable to find a plant growing north of its zone. The references may not have given it the right zone designation. There is also the possibility that some particularly favorable situation allows a plant to grow north of its zone — if so, that means there is a small island of that zone where a micro-zone exists. The center of large cities is an example. The maps do not reflect this "heat island" effect. In addition, what one may consider to be hardy, another may not. Think of a ground cover like pachysandra (*Pachysandra terminalis*). Its hardiness rating varies depending on whether you allow for the fact that snow usually covers and protects it in more northerly zones.

Seeds for Thought

Hardiness is an indicator of plant health and survival, rather than a guarantee of either success of failure. If you keep a few of these variables in mind, you're less likely to feel either tricked or betrayed by a plant's rating. Here's my own hardiness hint list:

- We can be in two zones at once.
- Plants may survive north of their zones.
- Plants rated for your zone may not survive; at the same time, plants not considered hardy may survive, either because of annual variations or micro-climates.
- Zone ratings are only approximate guides to a plant's northern limit of cold-hardiness.
- Hardiness will vary from the northern to the southern edge of a zone.
- Use the new USDA map as a guide to hardiness, and carefully check the zone ratings of plant stock or seeds, especially when purchasing from outside your own zone.

THE NORTHERN GARDENER'S LIBRARY

Chapter 3

Getting Started

Starting a New Garden

Raised-Bed Gardening

Vegetables to Consider

Gardening Under Lights

Herb Gardening

Container Gardening

Successful Tree Planting

Starting a New Garden

Kate Hintz

Looking back, the first garden I dug and planted was a fiasco. It was when I was in college. I was hungry for some fresh leaf lettuce and longing for a few flowers, so I went snooping around the basement of the house I was renting. I found an old, broken-handled shovel and went to the back field and started to dig. The rock-hard soil and I fought until, at about four inches, I gave up. The seeds went in and I waited for my garden to bloom and produce. The plants struggled through the summer and harvest time was disappointing to say the least.

Today I know better. The garden I started in my front yard in August got turned over to a depth of 12 to 15 inches. Cart loads of organic material were mixed into the soil. The plot grew two crops of buckwheat (a fast-growing, warm-season crop) that I also turned under in the course of the summer and fall. In the spring the plot was ready for plants. The soil is fertile and well-drained — conditions I have learned to be essential for plant and root growth. Whether you're growing petunias or peas,

chrysanthemums or calendulas, it all starts with the soil.

Getting started. As I learned, the process of making a new garden involves more than loosening the top few inches of soil. First draw up a plan that includes the size and shape of the plot and the desired plants. Since you will be entering the cultivated areas often to admire and tend the plants, be sure and include walkways in your plan to keep the compacted areas to a minimum.

Besides the plan, you will need an edger, a spade, a spading fork, compost or other organic material, edging material, a tarp, and a garden cart — not to mention time and perseverance.

Garden beds can be started in the spring, summer, or fall. If you have an abundance of decomposed organic material around to add to the soil, the garden you start in early spring could be ready to plant within a couple of days or weeks, depending on your energy level and the size of the plot.

Alternatively, if you would rather take your time, the bed you start in early summer will be ready for planting either in the fall or the following spring. You will have time to turn the soil and level it and plant a cover crop such as buckwheat. Cover crops not only add nitrogen and bulk to the soil, they also protect it from the elements and help control weeds. This scenario also allows you time to visit other people's gardens for inspiration before you commit plants to the ground.

Define the garden shape. Take your garden hose and snake it around to get a feel for the size and shape of the garden you have in mind. For irregular-shaped beds, this is all you will need for a guide. Rectangular or square beds can be marked out with stakes and string, then cut with your edger. To make a circular bed, hammer a stake into the ground and use a string as a compass to mark the perimeter of the garden. A rock "anchor" helps hold the string taut while you mark the shape.

Remove the sod. Once the perimeter of the garden is marked and cut, it is time to remove the sod. Cut rows of sod about a foot wide with your edger, then roll it back and sever the roots. In this manner, sod can be removed relatively quickly and cleanly.

If you want to remove some of the soil from the sod, let the sod sun-dry on a tarp and then shake out the loose soil. Sifting the soil will remove any remaining large roots. When you are done with the sod, haul it to your compost pile where it will make a great addition.

Remove the topsoil. Once the sod is gone, dig out about eight inches of topsoil and set it aside on a tarp. This step is a lot of work, but it allows access to the soil that will provide moisture and nutrients to the roots.

Add compost and other organic material. Organic material — such as compost, straw, decayed leaves, grass clippings, wood ashes, manure, or seaweed — should be mixed into the next eight to ten inches, turning the soil over with the spading fork. For this operation, dig a trough along one edge, add the organic material, and fork the next row of soil into the first row. Finally, rake the plot level.

This step is time-consuming, but it is critically important for sustained, productive gardening. The bulky organic material will hold moisture and make nutrients available to the plants over the next few years — this means sturdy stems, good flowers, and abundant roots in a light soil that holds water and yet drains well.

If you follow a few basic principles when starting out, a 'new' garden quickly becomes a healthy, 'established' garden. (MSHS)

Return the top soil to the garden. If the soil is sandy, mix in some peat moss at this time to improve the water-holding capacity. Likewise, if the soil is heavy, add peat moss or sand to loosen it up and improve the drainage. This is the time to add back any soil sifted from the sod.

Edge your garden bed. While the soil is still soft, install the edging material — a stone wall, railroad ties, conventional garden edging, or bricks. Walk ways should also be established at this time. You'll be entering the garden many times to plant and pick, and it would be a shame to compact the soil you just worked so hard to loosen up.

The garden is ready for planting — finally! The bountiful amount of organic material will allow the roots to explore for nutrients, water, and air — the essentials for prolific plant growth and flowering. If you consider a gardener's two main complaints — the soil and the weather — your new garden will have doubled its chances for success. You may not be able to do much about the weather, but changing the soil ensures it will help, not hinder, your efforts.

Raised-Bed Gardening

Dick Gray

If you have gardened for more than 50 years like I have, then you've undoubtedly tried various growing techniques from time to time. I've planted in everything from deeply-tilled soils to sod barely turned over. Some soils have been mulched, some fertilized, and some only furrowed before planting. I've used trellises, poles, wire frames, and strung wires for support. And I've had my share of problems: flooding, weeds, rabbits, chipmunks, raccoons, well-meaning dogs, wasps, and the general garden pests.

One fall , I decided to try to do something about all of the above, but wasn't sure what it would be until I happened to watch a gardening program on public television. The germ of an idea to try raised-bed gardening was formed. I haven't had a sorry moment since.

I suppose every gardener has had a raised bed of some sort at one time or another—including me—but having a whole garden with raised and contained beds was new to me.

I took a sheet of graph paper and started to lay out a new gar-den. First I was stuck with my raspberries and grapes in their permanent positions. Secondly I had to decide the optimum widths and lengths of the special beds that I wanted. I decided raspberries should be in two-foot wide beds and grapes in four-foot widths. Furthermore, I decided there should be two-foot walkways between beds with five feet between the grape rows. Another arbitrary decision was to make all of the new beds on four-foot modules: 4' x 4', 4' x 8', 4' x 16', etc. The remaining decision was how to make the beds.

I discussed my needs with a friend who does landscape consulting, and between us we worked out the procedure for establishing a series of raised beds in the garden. Each bed was contained in a framework of 2" x 10" redwood planks which were installed with six inches below ground and four inches above. The walkways between beds were lined with plastic sheeting and covered with pea gravel. New soil was hauled in after the main sides to the garden plot were raised, using railroad-tie timbers to build

These raised beds provide plenty of growing space in this northern garden. Pathways between beds make them easy to maintain and allow plenty of access. (MSHS)

the entire garden above possible flooding levels. (The garden has always been barely above lake or groundwater level.)

The new garden layout was finished before a hard freeze late in the fall. It was with great anticipation that I awaited the first planting of "cold" things on the spring weekend when the ice would go out on our lake. I have found over a period of nearly 50 years that ice-out and first vegetable seed plantings go together.

On a mid-April weekend, radishes, peas, beets, onion sets, and lettuce were seeded outdoors in the new raised beds. By the third week in May, the "hot" seeds of beans, cucumbers, squash, and flowers were planted, and transplants of seeds started indoors—the eggplant, peppers, and varieties of cabbage—were set out.

Overall, I planted 19 varieties of vegetables and flowers. Peppers, eggplant, and cabbage plants were laid in the raised beds on one-foot centers in 4' x 4' beds. In other words, nine plants were grown in an area of 4' x 4' feet. Row vegetables like carrots, onions, beets, beans, and the like were planted with three rows per four-foot width. The rows could be mixed—radishes with lettuce, beans with beets, etc. Depending upon the amount of a vegetable that I wanted, I used four, eight, or twelve-foot-long beds. For instance, in one

4' x 8' bed, I had an eight-foot row of green beans, an eight-foot row of yellow beans, and an eight-foot row of mixed zinnias.

Harvesting the produce is the final test, and I was swamped with results. Carrots were long and perfect, cucumbers firm and straight, cabbages hard and well-formed. Everything grew well.

In spite of terrible rains and flooding, the garden was dry and workable at all times. Even after a hard rain, I could immediately walk around in the garden on the gravel paths and cultivate, easily reaching any row because nothing was more than two feet away from a gravel path and ready access. The raised sides of the garden success-fully kept rabbits and chipmunks out without fencing. Dusting was simple after a rain, and pest control hasn't been a problem.

Now after years of successful gardening using raised beds, I have found several distinct advantages that weren't readily apparent. Each bed can be watered in varying amounts depending upon the plants. Each can be fertilized in varying amounts and in different ratios. Each can be sprayed or dust-ed at the best time with its proper pesticide. Cultivating can be done a little at a time, one bed at a time, rain or shine. A great way to garden!

Patio areas lend themselves to raised-bed flower gardening. These beds are constructed from 2" x 10" wooden planks dropped slightly below the brick line. (MSHS)

Vegetables to Consider

Lawrence Rule

If you're just starting out with a vegetable garden, the important thing is to realize just what a range of vegetable varieties exist, and start looking at the experiences of other gardeners and your own preferences. This listing of vegetable varieties is not complete, but it does include most of the vegetables that have proven to be outstanding for me in terms of both performance and quality.

One of the easiest, yet most productive steps to raising better vegetables is to sit back in your easy chair in winter, surrounded by catalogs from reputable seed dealers, and take the time to read the prose, as well as sigh at the beautiful, color pictures. But don't sigh too long — seeds should be ordered early. Along with those varieties that have been faithful over the years, try some of the newest introductions. The absolute worst way to select your seeds is to wait until you are ready to plant and then race out to the nearest hardware store and purchase a big selection of whatever is left on the rack.

When selecting seed, there are many things to keep in mind. Look for varieties which are disease resistant. With our short growing season, it is important to consider the days from seeding or transplanting to harvest. The number in parentheses after each variety mentioned refers to growing season. For example, (48s) means harvest began 48 days after seeding in the garden, while (48t) would mean harvest began 48 days after transplanting into the garden.

Order hybrid varieties when possible. Look for seed dealers who are courageous enough to treat susceptible seeds, such as snap beans and sweet corn, against damping off. The money you spend on seeds will give you the greatest return of any expense in your garden, so buy only the best.

Asparagus

My asparagus patch is well established with a 'Mary Washington' strain; however, I will be watching some of the newer, numbered strains that are showing promise. If you're starting a new patch, you might consider one of those.

Snap Beans

'Contender' (48s) and the new 'Venture' (48s) are early bearers and they resist cool weather. 'Bush Blue Lake' (55s) is hard to beat for quality and production. 'Sungold' (56s) and 'Slenderwax' (56s) have small, disciplined bushes and beans that are a delightful yellow. The old-fashioned 'Kentucky Wonder' has long, lumpy pods and is available in both pole and bush types; many people like its "beany" flavor. My favorite pole bean is 'Romano' (65s) which bears fairly large, flat bean pods of a distinctive taste when planted about the first of June.

Beets

I don't think the best beet has been discovered yet, so I limp along with 'Ruby Ball' (55s).

Broccoli

'Packman' (60t) bears early and produces side shoots throughout the growing season. 'Green Valiant' (83t) is a late variety that has larger heads and offers side shoots up until a hard freeze.

Brussels Sprouts

'Prince Marvel' (98t) has done very well for me. The sprouts are best if harvested after a frost or two.

Cabbage

'Ruby Ball' (70t) is still the best early red cabbage. Though the heads resist splitting, it does become inedible if left in the summer patch too long. Two very early varieties, 'Darkri' and 'Spivoy', were harvested less than 50 days after being transplanted into my garden. Both should produce heads under two pounds. 'Spivoy,' as you can imagine, has savoyed leaves. 'Market Victor' (65t) is a nice, round, blue-green cabbage, and 'King Cole' (68t) is suitable for most of our short summers. 'Savoy King' (86t) is a good late savoyed cabbage with poor storage ability. 'Danish Ball Head' (90t) matures in the fall. These two can easily grow 10 pound heads — too large for many families.

Chinese Cabbage

'Two Seasons Hybrid' (62s) Chinese cabbage was introduced in 1987. It proved to be quite versatile. Our family used it as a salad green, in cole slaw, and as the main ingredient in stir-fry dishes. The spring transplants resisted bolting (going to seed), and were harvested from the middle of June until July 26. The fall crop was seeded in the garden the first of July, and produced from August 16 until the last head was harvested October 12.

Carrots

'A-Plus' (70s) is the carrot to which all others are compared. This cultivar is orange in color, sweet, tender, and coreless. It is also high in vitamin A. Make several plantings of 'A-Plus' and use it before it is fully developed. 'Toudo' (70s) is an excellent carrot if used when it is about the size of your middle finger.

Swiss Chard

Chard will provide you with greens through the hot summer months and into fall. If you use the outside leaves, production will be non-stop. 'Lucillus' (60s) is light green, tender, and mild. 'Rhubarb Chard' (60s) will give you a deep red, colorful show in the garden, and on your plate. Some chard will go to seed — relegate it to the compost pile, if this happens to yours.

Cucumbers

'Salad Bush' (60s) is handy in the small garden, since its small vines extend less than three feet. Despite its size, however, the vine will present you with a lot of dark green, well-formed slicers for early summer use. 'Sweet Success' (58s) will bear very early if started indoors. If you are after straight fruit, it's best to trellis the vines. If planted in the absence of other cucumbers, they will be virtually seedless. Other excellent slicers, especially when trellised, are 'Elite' (60s) and 'Marketmore 76' (67s). All but 'Salad Bush', if kept picked, should continue to produce until frost.

Cauliflower

'Snow Crown' (53t) is a dependable early variety, but it needs to be tied as soon as a curd develops. To date, I have not found a satisfactory cauliflower for fall harvest.

Eggplant

If you are growing just one eggplant, make it 'Dusky' (60t). It is a very good, all-around choice. I've also tried the recently introduced 'Early Bird' (50t). It was of usable size nine days before 'Dusky', however, the fruit was smaller.

'Salad Bush' is perfect for limited-space gardens, patio planters or containers. (AAS)

Kohlrabi

'Grand Duke' (5Os) is as good as any, but 'Purple Danube' (46s) is more handsome in the garden.

Leek

Start 'Giant Musselburgh' (90t) as a transplant, and with lots of care, they may grow as big as baseball bats by October.

Lettuce

Cos or Romaine is a favorite lettuce of our household, and I like the looks and taste of 'Green Towers' (74s), a 1987 introduction. 'Black Seeded Simpson' (45s) is a good, yellow-green leaf lettuce for spring and fall. 'Salad Bowl' (45s) is useable in midsummer. 'Red Sails' (45s) is a colorful companion to green leaf lettuce, and is productive in spring, summer, and fall. 'Buttercrunch' (60s) may be the finest of lettuces for spring and fall butter-heads. I find head lettuce can be grown here, but isn't it enough to eat this the rest of the year? You might try growing 'Buttercrunch' under fluorescent lights this winter. All lettuce can be seeded indoors and transplanted into the garden for an earlier start.

Muskmelons

With peat pot transplants and the use of plastic, you can grow some fine muskmelons in the North. I relish 'Burpee Hybrid' (82s), 'Superstar' (82s), and 'Dixie Jumbo' (85s). The first two are capable of producing large fruit. Try 'Honey Drip' (85s) to replace 'Earlidew' for your honeydew melon. 'Alaska' (75s) is a heavy-bearing, earlier melon, but lacks the sweetness of some of the others, such as 'Dixie Jumbo'.

Onions

Unless you grow your onions from seeds, you do not get much of a selection. On the other hand, it may not be worth your effort to mess with seeds. 'Stuttgarter' sets will provide you with scallions early, and still serve well as a storage onion. Yellow Sweet Spanish plants produce large, sweet onions, but they do not store well.

Peas

There are a lot of sugar snap types of peas on the market. With these peas, you wait until the pod is plump with peas, and then eat it, pod and all. One of the good, new varieties is 'Sugar Mel' (68s), which has a large pod on a three-foot vine. Chinese or snow peas are eaten for the pods before the peas develop. 'Oregon Sugar Pod II' (65s) has thick, tender pods, growing on a vine only two feet tall. English peas are grown for the peas, which are harvested when developed, but still tender, in the pods. 'Knight' (62s) and 'Patriot' (62s) grow nicely on a two-foot chicken-wire fence.

Peas grow best during cool weather. Make your first planting as soon as the soil can be worked. Sugar Peas have tender, edible pods. (AAS)

Peppers

At present, 'Lady Bell' (72t) is my favorite sweet pepper. 'New Ace' (60t) may bear several days earlier, but it is thinner walled. A new hot pepper in 1988 was 'Super Chili' (60t). This little bush is covered with small, upright peppers which eventually turn fiery red. One bite of these and you will be blowing smoke for 30 minutes.

Potatoes

Potatoes grown from seeds are still a gimmick. Seed catalogs sell "seed eyes," but the best bet is to find a place selling a variety of certified seed potatoes. 'Norland Red' is a good quality, early red potato, and 'Norgold Russett' is an excellent mid-season potato. The home gardener should plant 'Norland Red' to have peas and new potatoes on the table at the same time.

Pumpkin

'Jackpot' (100s) and 'Autumn Gold' (90s) are my favorites. 'Jackpot' is a bush type, much like summer squash. It is smooth, well-shaped, orange, and medium-sized. 'Autumn Gold', a 1987 All-America Selection, begins to have its pumpkin color as soon as the fruit forms on the vine. The fruit is round and about eight inches in diameter. It should have time to ripen nearly everywhere in Minnesota. Too bad it has such a trailing vine. Both 'Jackpot' and

'Autumn Gold' are good for carving and decorating. I wouldn't know about their eating qualities.

Radish

There are many "cherry-type" radishes, and most of them are good. Worth trying is 'Crimson Giant' (26s), a shiny, dark red radish that can grow to the size of a golf ball without getting pithy. It does best when grown as a fall crop. If you have deep sandy or loamy soil, you will want to try 'Summer Season' (45s). Seed it to mature in summer or fall; you may be surprised by the snow-white radishes, two feet long, which, despite their size, are sweet.

Spinach

'Melody' (43s) does well in spring, but it is especially fine as a fall crop. Try New Zealand Spinach (55s) as a midsummer substitute for the salad or steamer, even though it is not even related to spinach.

Summer Squash

There are many excellent varieties of zucchini, all being productive. 'Black Magic' and 'Spineless' differ from the rest, in that there are no spines on the leaves. (I never even thought about spines until these came onto the market!) 'Gold Rush' looks like it just had a wax job, and the golden fruit is easy to spot amid the leaves.

How many ways can you prepare summer squash? You'll need lots of recipes because home-grown summer squash is delicious and highly productive. (MSHS)

Winter Squash

'Table Ace' (75s) is often sold as a bush squash, but for me it has overly venturesome vines. It is the uniform fruit, sweet and lack of stringiness, that has us sold on 'Table Ace'. The squash is about the right size for two people. 'Sweet Mama' (90s) has flesh that is sweet and dry like 'Buttercup', but matures sooner; expect a heavy crop of squash in the five- to eight-pound range. They store well — we are generally able to save one for Easter.

Sweet Corn

If you enjoy the extra-sweet varieties, be sure to try 'Honey 'N Pearl' (78s), a bi-colored corn introduced in 1988 and an All-America Selection winner. The ears are large and tender. 'How Sweet It Is' (78s) is my favorite, however, and was an All-America Selection in 1986. The small, white kernels are produced on large ears of 14 to 16 rows. They hold their sweetness even after they are mature for a week on the stalk.

For best results, separate your extra-sweet corn by geography or time of harvest from other sweet corn varieties.

Tomatoes

Small, early tomatoes can be harvested from such compact, determinate plants as 'Pixie' (52t) and 'Early Temptation' (48t).

When planning your garden, know what you want and how much. (Fischer)

'Cascade' (54t) and 'Early Pik' (62t) should mature even in the northern part of the state. 'Avalanche' (72t), 'Jet Star, (72t) and 'Ultra Girl' (70t) are excellent mid-season, indeterminate varieties. The last five mentioned do well in cages, and 'Jet Star' yields a good crop staked, as well as caged.

Watermelons

'Sugar Baby' (80s) is a dependable, little watermelon which, though early, is still about as sweet as any. 'Yellow Baby' (80s) is an early, sweet, small melon which, as you guessed, has yellow flesh.

Gardening Skill

Better Tomatoes

• Seed your own tomatoes only if you have a good light source.

• Whether you seed or purchase plants, choose one of two early hybrid varieties and one or two medium season varieties. Stay away from varieties that take over 75 days to ripen.

• Grow only those hybrids that are developed for resistance to tomato diseases. Good seed catalogs will list both growing time and resistance to fungus, viral, and bacterial diseases. Expensive hybrid seed is money well spent.

• Move your crops around each year in the garden to help prevent disease. Also, discard any diseased plants; do not add diseased material to the compost pile.

• Ready your vegetable bed in the fall with a good general fertilizer well worked into the soil with leaf compost or other soil conditioners.

• If a spring feeding is used, nitrogen should be used only early in June. From July on, feed a low or no nitrogen food mix. Liquid solution works fast for such a short season. Use 5-20-20 solid food, 9-45-30 or 10-30-20 liquid food.

• Tie your plants or cage them if space is limited. Let the single main stem be the one growing leader.

• If we have a damp season, spray with a fungicide such as Zineb to prevent later fungus problems.

• Mulch your plants to keep soil moist. Don't go from over-wet to overly dry extremes. Don't hoe around the plants after the first week or two. Tomatoes have shallow feeder roots which hoeing destroys.

• Be sure to collar the stem after transplanting.

Seeds for Thought

Transplanting Tips

Transplanting seedlings into the garden always shocks young plants, but there are methods that cause plants to suffer minimal setback or growth delay. Deborah Brown of the University Agricultural Extension Service provides these suggestions:

- Start when plants are small. Annual or vegetable seedlings with four to six leaves are big enough to move.

- Transplant at sundown or on a cloudy day; wind can be as damaging as sunlight.

- Water seedlings thoroughly several hours before transplanting.

- Move seedlings with as much soil as possible around the roots.

- Plant seedlings a little lower than the surrounding soil. This forms a depression to hold water.

- Plants in degradable pots, such as peat pots or pellets, should be planted with their containers below the garden soil surface, to keep them from drying out.

- Water the soil around each transplant as soon as it is in the ground, and include a diluted starter fertilizer, made by dissolving one-half cup of 5-10-5 or 5-10-10 fertilizer in a gallon of water. Use about one-half cup of the diluted mixture for each transplant.

Gardening Under Lights

Fred Glasoe and Robert E. Kelly

The gardening year truly begins in late October and early November. As frost advances, every outdoor plant in the colder climates dies or puts itself to bed for the winter. We, as gardeners, start to get ready for next summer. In our yard, we clean up debris, fertilize and turn the soil, and tuck a few tulips and lilies into earthen beds.

Soon the seed catalogs start arriving and are carefully studied, which means comparing prices and deciding whether or not to order this season's crop of new wonders. I can almost feel the spring sunshine when I visualize the first wave of seedlings for next summer's garden. Most of my winter indoor work is getting plants ready for the outdoor landscape. I hate babysitting too many pots of indoor greenery, especially those which give little color to the winter scene, and therefore little satisfaction. The great reward of outdoor planting is seeing the colorful bloom of plants which I have grown myself from tiny seeds. Every year, the miracle repeats itself and faith is rewarded, as seeds first become seedlings and then mature plants with beautiful, showy blooms and fruit.

Fluorescent lights have made it possible for gardeners to have a fine and worthwhile winter hobby. Windowsill and home greenhouse growing isn't always practical in the north with the lack of energy from the sun in midwinter. Light is the most important seedling stimulus, and fluorescent tubes have made it abundantly available and easy to regulate. Everyone can get a good garden started under a two- or four-tube fluorescent light fixture. The cost is nominal and the construction of a fluorescent-lighted area is very simple. A fixture, a chain to change the height of the tubes, a timer, and a tray to hold some saturated media which will provide humidity, are the necessary ingredients. After the seeds have germinated in a warm area of the house, a cool basement or workshop is usually just right for growing short, strong-stemmed transplants.

I use a combination of regular warm white and cool white 40-watt fluorescent tubes. I have better luck with these ordinary tubes than with special, more expensive grow lights. After planting the seeds in a good, sterile seeding medium, such as light potting soil or a special seeding mix, place the seed trays only three to four inches beneath the fluorescent tubes. Later, when the plants are transplanted to pots, the lights can be raised to five to eight inches above the plants, and later ten to twelve inches. Never move the light source more than 12 inches from the seedlings, and leave them on for 16 to 18 hours a day.

Centrally heated homes do not usually produce the humid conditions favored by most plants. I set my trays and pots on a synthetic rock called Turface. This porous material holds about 10 times its weight in water, which evaporates upwards, surrounding the plant pots and seed boxes. Plants enjoy this evaporation and prosper. The rock holds the seed containers above the water, which remains just below the rock level in the fiberglass holding trays. By hanging large sheets of aluminum foil from the sides of the light fixtures, humidity is retained around the plants, and additional light is reflected onto the growing area. Materials such as sand or gravel can also be used in the holding trays, but I have found Turface superior because of its coarseness and water retentiveness.

By mid-January I like to get my geraniums well underway. They are easy to grow and although the seeds seem expensive, a hundred plants can be grown for the price of just a few greenhouse plants. A January start gives me early spring-blooming indoor plants, which are growing well even before the February sowings of a few small-seeded annuals, like petunias, heliotrope and begonias.

Starting the Annual Flower Garden

February's other main task is to complete your seed catalog orders. Let's assume that you are eager to try growing annuals from seed, starting with varieties that caught your fancy in catalogs. Order early; if you wait for spring you will have to plant directly into the outdoor garden and be satisfied with less (and much later) bloom.

When the seeds arrive, they will vary in size from the large zinnia seeds (3,000 to 5,000 per ounce) to begonias whose seeds count 2,000,000 to the ounce. Seeding trays, filled with a mixture of Jiffy mix, perlite, and sand in equal proportion, placed under four-foot fluorescent light tubes in a warm, well-ventilated area of your home, will give your seedlings a good start. After the first set of true leaves appears, you can transplant the seedlings into plastic pots containing a mixture of one-third sterilized soil, one-third perlite, and one-third peat. The proper time to start seeds is different for each variety, but the big push will come in March; by the first of April, everything should be out of the trays and in pots. The trick is to allow the plants to get big enough to give you a good head start in the garden, without outgrowing their pots before transplanting. Fertilize approximately every 10 days with a liquid, low nitrogen (9-45-15) solution that is diluted to about one-quarter strength.

An important step for your plants on the way to the garden is a week to 10-day adjustment period in a coldframe. Remember that the plants need to be hardened off, getting accustomed first to a few days in the shade, then gradually to more sun, while still spending their nights indoors. By mid-May, when all danger of frost has passed, you will have many plants to set out, will have saved much money by not buying plants, and best of all, you'll have a much wider selection of plants than offered by your local nursery or garden center.

As for choice of plants and varieties, beauty is in the eye of the beholder. Impatiens and marigolds have edged out petunias in popularity, and geraniums are coming up fast. Impatiens from New Guinea are now more sun tolerant, and Japan is producing many hybrid flowers and vegetables. Central America, particularly Costa

By seeding your own salvia, you can afford a field of beautiful blue spires. (MSHS)

Rica, has a year round summer climate which produces an abundance of flowers and seeds. Development of first generation hybrids (F1) has made annuals more vigorous and floriferous. A little more costly because they must be propagated by hand, these hybrids are infinitely more productive.

Here are a few choices from our order blank that we've found to be effective, both in terms of seedling growth and display in the garden.
Celosia: Geisha Mix (dwarf)
Cosmos: Klondike Mix
Dahlia: Unwin Hybrid Mix (double dwarf)
Geraniums: Showgirl, Red

Sprinter, White Sprinter, Coral
Orbit

Helichrysum: (Strawflower)
Double Mix

Impatiens: Blitz Violet

Lobelia: Blue Gown, Rainbow
Cascade

Nicotiana: Nicki Mix

Primula: Ducat F_1 Mix, Julian
Bicolor

Ranunculus: Bloomingdale Mix F_1

Salvia: Blue Victoria, Royal
Mountie

Snapdragon: Coronette Mix,
Carioca Mix

Thunbergia: Susie Mix

Marigolds and petunias offer the most choices, and most are good. Don't forget that ornamental vegetables are a nice counterpoint in the flower garden. We like accents of flowering kale, ornamental basil, and 'Candlelight' ornamental pepper. If you have a large background area, you might grow castor bean. We have grown it to 10 feet tall. This is a poisonous plant, but quite exotic.

Creating Perennial Blooms from Seed

Many people don't seem to realize that perennials, as well as annuals and vegetables, can be started from seed in midwinter for planting outdoors in the spring. It is true that some of these seeds must be handled in different and sometimes more complicated ways that most of our favorite annuals, but with a little care and pre-planting investigation, it can be done.

Hardy phlox, astilbe, rudbeckias, painted daisy, veronica, monarda, many varieties of poppy, hardy hibiscus, gaillardia, lupines, mums, dianthus, and delphiniums are only a few of the perennials you can grow under lights during the gray days of winter. You'll have fun with them, and you'll also appreciate what growing them from seeds will do to your pocketbook. Your greatest reward comes in being able to afford an entire bed or grouping of a perennial which most gardeners grow individually or in pairs. Imagine a four-foot display of blue, violet, or

Early summer blooming lupines are a good choice for starting under lights. (MSHS)

white delphiniums, or an entire bed of multi-colored lupines in June. If you raise more plants than you need, donate them to a garden club sale or give them to a few happy friends who will admire your outstanding green thumb. They'll appreciate knowing someone who grows whole flats of perennials, which retail at the greenhouse for three or four dollars per plant.

Most good seed houses carry a wide variety of perennial seeds and also furnish good culture sheets with special instructions, telling you when and how to plant and grow each variety. Order early because some of the seeds need to be pre-cooled and started between December and early February to insure first-year blooms.

Perennial seedlings demand long days and short nights. A good quality timer is a must for your lighting operation. Germination of some seeds can be accelerated with 24 hours of light, while other seeds germinate best in total darkness. Check the culture sheets furnished with the seeds or the information in the seed catalog.

Most seeds need a warm temperature (70°) for germination, but will grow better under cooler conditions. Incandescent light bulbs or heating cables can provide the extra heat during germination. After the first transplant from seed trays to individual pots, an unfin-ished basement usually provides about the right temperature (55°-60°) for growth of the seedlings.

The plants may require a second transplant into larger individual pots by early spring. As the perennial grows, it can be pinched back and developed into a good, strong, bushy plant, ready for a cold frame or slow conditioning into the outdoor environment in early May. Plants can be popped into their permanent home in the garden a few weeks later.

Growing plants under lights during the dark winter days can help eliminate that gray, melancholy winter feeling. Doing your own seeding helps you get acquainted with new and better plant varieties. New colors and tastes can be thrills for the entire family. Too often we depend on other growers to get our garden plants started, and that can mean the same old varieties and the same small selection year after year. Some winters, my garden under lights becomes as much fun as the big summer garden outside. By mid-March many of our seedlings have been transplanted and repotted, developing into sturdy plants for April and May plantings. Meanwhile, we enjoy every day of fluorescent brightness in our basement. There's nothing quite as fresh and new as our garden of tiny seedlings.

Herb Gardening

Lina Belar and
Mary Grommesh Bydlon

Growing your own herbs can become a delightful adventure in itself, with the bonus of providing an added dimension and elegance to your cooking. Nothing compares to being able to walk through you own herb garden, purposely brushing the plants to release their distinct aromas. The fragrance of herbs has no equal.

Spring is the time of the year to be thinking of growing your own herbs. Special herb gardening areas are not needed. Herbs will thrive in a vegetable garden, in and around flower beds, or in pots on the patio. Herb plants are not fussy, although they like lots of sun and well-drained soil. Some of them are susceptible to frost. In the north, therefore, plan to plant after the last frost, usually the end of May.

If you have a choice, plant your herbs as close to the kitchen door as possible. Fresh herbs can be used every day, but if they are too far away, many meals will be served without these delightful seasoning accents.

Before you purchase seed or plants, have a plan and plant only those you intend to use. If you are just beginning to use herbs, plant the more popular culinary herbs, a few the first year, then plan to add one or two or more each year.

One of the pleasures of having an herb garden is being able to have fresh herbs on hand at all times. Harvesting of home-grown herb plants can begin almost immediately. As the spring plants grow, snip off some of the new growth, not only for kitchen use but also to promote a bushier plant.

As the plants mature and you find a surplus of new growth (about midsummer) it is time to harvest in quantity. Herb flavors are more concentrated just before the plant comes into blossom. On a sunny morning after the dew has dried, cut the tops from the herb plants you wish to harvest; cut only as many as you can handle before they wilt. Rinse them quickly in slightly warm water and blot gently between paper or cloth towels.

If you can't use them right away, herb cuttings can be dried or frozen for later use. For drying tie the herbs together in small bunches and hang, stems up, in a dark, well-ventilated area until crispy-dry. After drying store the herbs in air-tight jars in a dark place. Do not store in full light near the kitchen range; light and heat destroy herb color and flavor.

To freeze fresh herbs, place about one to three teaspoons of the herb on squares of aluminum foil and wrap tightly. Or freeze small amounts of individual herbs in water in ice cube trays. Frozen cubes can be emptied into a freezer bag, labeled, dated, and stored in the freezer.

As you begin to use herbs, be aware that there are dominant herbs and blending herbs. Dominant herbs (such as sage, rosemary, tarragon and thyme) have robust, pronounced flavors. They are generally used alone, not in combination. Blending herbs (such as chervil, parsley, chives, basil, marjoram, and summer savory) may be used alone or in combination. Herb flavors should enhance food, not overwhelm.

If you are new to using herbs, use only one herb at a time. Do not combine flavors with a second herb until you are familiar with the first herb flavor. There is a difference between fresh and dried herbs. Dried herbs are more concentrated, about three times stronger in flavor than fresh herbs. (Recipes are usually written using dried herbs unless specified.

Therefore, if using your own fresh herbs, use three times as much as the recipe requires.)

Herbs are a cook's friend. Experiment with them. Learn to recognize the different flavors. You will soon have your own favorites. Herbs can perk up not only your meals but also your spirits. Once you have used fresh herbs or those you have dried yourself, especially those you have grown in your own garden, you will be convinced there is no other way to season food.

Knowing a little bit about the different culinary herbs and their cultural preferences will help you decide which ones you'd like to include in your garden or green-house, or even your kitchen win-dowsill.

Arugula, also called rocket, is a leafy green herb with a spicy, pep-pery flavor that will add excite-ment to any salad. It is ready to harvest in about six weeks from seed, as are most of the annual herbs, and the leaves can be taken from the plant much as you'd har-vest leaf lettuce. Arugula demands cool weather and low light, so a cool, shady location is a good choice for this herb.

Another herb for the cool shade is **chervil**. This fine-leaved herb looks at first glance like parsley, but it has a slight licorice flavor and is widely used in French cooking in salad dressings, egg dishes, and sauces for chicken and fish.

Coriander, when grown for its leaves rather than seeds, should also be given a cool, shady location; otherwise it will bolt and go to seed too quickly. Also called cilantro or Chinese parsley, coriander is an aromatic herb, with a rather peculiar scent when fresh and a remarkably different aroma when dried. It is widely used in both Chinese and Mexican cooking, and is one of the bitter herbs of Passover.

On the other end of the light spectrum are the **basils**. They like lots of light and heat. Often called the "queen of herbs," basil comes in many forms, the most familiar being the large, green-leaved sweet basil. Also available are opal basil, lemon basil, licorice basil, and cinnamon basil, to name just a few. Basil is a must in tomato sauce and Italian cooking.

If basil is queen, then **mint** should surely be king. There are a number of different kinds of mint, from the harsh wild mint found in the woods to the flavorful peppermint made famous by Wrigley's. Mint tea is a refreshing drink, hot or cold, and mint leaves are used widely in fruit salads, fish sauces, and mint sauce for lamb. Mint is a perennial and will come up every year with a little winter protection. It spreads quite easily by runners, so be sure to contain your mint bed or it will invade its neighbors. Spearmint is the most commonly grown mint, but peppermint, apple-mint, orange-mint, and many others are also available.

Sweet fennel, or finocchio, is a licorice-flavored herb most commonly grown to maturity, at which point it resembles a rather fat celery clump. The young, tender shoots are delicious in salads and rice dishes. Try cooking onions with chopped fennel — it will make them sweeter. Seed it directly in the garden and don't bother to thin. Just cut what you need and reseed.

Dill is widely used in cheese dips, fish sauce, and potato salad. Cut it while it is still young and feathery, and seed a little each week in order to have a continuous crop.

French sorrel, as distinct from the sorrel that is found growing wild, has large leaves with a lemon flavor. They are wonderful to use in a salad, and a classic French sorrel soup, good hot or cold, is made from this herb. This plant likes lots of moisture. Harvest it as you would leaf lettuce; it will keep producing indefinitely. Grow it easily from seeds.

Chives are very common. If you let them go to seed, they may become even more common than you wish. Although they like lots of moisture, they will tolerate most conditions. The flowers are lovely and can be used to make chive-flavored vinegar.

French tarragon does not grow from seed, only cuttings. If you find tarragon seeds, they are Russian tarragon, an undesirable herb. French tarragon is a lovely plant and quite hardy here. Cut it all summer long but not too far back or you might trigger dormancy. You can keep pots growing all winter under lights, but let them rest in the spring when the outdoor tarragon begins. Propagate tarragon from a bit of the root. Tarragon is wonderful in salads, fish dishes, eggs, and a must in Bearnaise sauce.

Rosemary is a lovely plant to

Chives are a very hardy addition to the herb garden. (MHSH)

grow all year indoors. It is hardy to only 15°F. Set it outside in the summer along with your hardier houseplants. To propagate rosemary, take a piece of the new growth along with a little heel of the old wood. Tear it off the plant rather than clip it. Stick it in a sterile potting mixture and cover it with a bag to make a mini-greenhouse. It will root in two to three weeks. Watch that the moisture does not get too high, or it will rot before it roots. Rosemary is a lovely aromatic herb, excellent with beef and pork. A little goes a long way, since it is quite strong.

Sage is another herb that is particularly good with fatty meats and fish, as well as cheese and rice. Grow it in full sun in well-drained conditions, from seeds started early indoors. There are many varieties besides the common garden sage — colorful red sage, green and gold variegated sage, tricolor sage (tinged with red), and the fragrant pineapple sage.

Marjoram, oregano, and thyme can be propagated from cuttings, but they are also very easily grown from seed. Put a little pinch of seeds in a small pot and when the seedlings are large enough, move to a bigger pot or plant outside. Sometimes, oregano and thyme will overwinter in zone 4, but they are not reliably hardy.

Oregano is a very popular herb in Italian cooking and widely used in spaghetti sauce, pizza, chili, and with meat dishes. The Greek strain is more pungent, but the common oregano is a more attractive plant.

Thyme comes in all shapes and sizes, and there is also a lemon thyme that has a delightful aroma. Choose the thyme that best suits your garden. Use it in meat and fish dishes, in soup and chowders. Like rosemary, thyme is a pretty dominant herb, so use just a little.

Marjoram is much milder, but still delightfully pungent. It's good in soups and salads, with roast lamb or boiled fish, and with peas or beans.

There is **summer savory** and **winter savory**; both grow in the summer. The winter savory is woodier and stronger flavored. Savory is very good in meat dishes, poultry stuffing, and with string beans.

Lemon balm is another very attractive plant and it, too, is sometimes perennial. Grow it easily from seed or cuttings. It has a mint and lemon flavor combination and makes a refreshing iced tea. Use it like mint in salads, as well as with rice or eggs.

Parsley comes either curled or flat. The curled type is the attractive garnish most people leave on their plates at a restaurant. The flat-leaved, or Italian, parsley is a little stronger flavored. Both make an attractive plant for indoors or out.

Nasturtiums are a wonderful

You can use both the foliage and flowers of nasturium. (MSHS)

addition to the herb garden because of their lovely flowers. They have a uniquely sweet and peppery flavor. You can eat both the leaves and the flowers. To promote flowering, stress them. In other words, all the things you shouldn't do to your plants — like underwatering and underfeeding — will make nasturtiums produce more flowers. They need lots of light for best flower production.

There are many other herbs worthy of note, but these are the main ones used in cooking and an excellent mix for a garden.

Container Gardening

Margaret Haapoja

In the northern states many of us must contend with the problem of sandy soil when planting our gardens. And although we in the northern states are often blessed with beautiful evergreens and other shade trees in our yards, these too can present problems if we wish to grow sunny annuals. To solve these problems of poor soil and too much shade, you may want to try container gardening.

Many types of containers can be used, including the popular redwood tubs that are weather resistant and durable. Attractive plastic containers are available, some of which are impossible to tell apart in appearance from clay pots. We have made yard planters out of hollowed-out tree stumps; these planters may not appeal to everyone, but they look natural in our wooded setting. Hanging baskets are a special category of containers which provide an effective way of brightening overhead spaces on a deck, patio, or entryway.

No matter what type of container you use, be sure it provides adequate drainage. Wooden pots or tubs should have holes drilled in the bottom. Clay pots are porous and dry out so rapidly that it is advisable to use a plastic pot as a liner. Plastic tubs or hanging baskets usually have drainage holes in the bottom and a saucer underneath.

Container gardening demands a special soil mix, one able to hold water and nutrients even through hot, dry weather. We mix our own,

This coleus is positioned to catch filtered sunlight. (Carlson)

screening it into a wheelbarrow through a framed piece of one-half inch mesh screening. My recipe calls for one part peat moss; one part compost, well-rotted manure, or leaf mold; one part garden soil; and at least one shovelful of builders' sand. I usually add a handful of bone meal to each container.

The best candidates for container culture are annuals and tender perennials that usually have shallow roots and long flowering seasons. Petunias are one of the most popular flowers for container growth; however, they often become leggy and ragged-looking by midsummer. For a one-variety container, the best choices are geraniums, dwarf marigolds, wax begonias, impatiens, verbenas, dwarf zinnias, and tuberous begonias. Hanging baskets look best if they contain only matched plants so that the effect is of one large plant. (Three to five plants may be needed to give this full look.) Impatiens are a good choice for hanging baskets, as are fuschias, petunias, and the trailing type of tuberous begonias.

There are more advantages than disadvantages to container gardening, but there is one important drawback: increased maintenance. Plants in containers need both water and fertilizer more regularly than plants growing in a garden bed. I feed my pots and baskets

Impatiens are a good choice for one-variety container plantings. (Wehrwein)

every other week with a solution of water and water-soluble fertilizer. Depending on the size of the container, the heat, and the humidity, you may have to water several times a week or even every day. Potted plants also need special watching to keep them looking their best. They should be pruned if they start to lose their shape, and fading flowers should be removed to improve appearance and prevent loss of vigor.

Following is a listing of plants suitable for container gardening.

FLOWER A—ANNUAL B—BIENNIAL P—PERENNIAL[1] TP—TENDER PERENNIAL[2]		HANGING BASKET	TUB OR 2 TO 5 GALLON CONTAINER	LARGE CONTAINER 8-12 INCH POT	SMALL CONTAINER 4-6 INCH POT	FULL SUN	PARTIAL SHADE	FULL SHADE
Achimenes	TP	•			•	•		•
Ageratum	A				•	•	•	
Alyssum	P	•			•			•
Alyssum, Sweet	A	•				•	•	•
Aster	A				•	•	•	
Balsam	A				•	•	•	
Begonia	TP	•				•	•	•
Browallia	A	•				•	•	•
Calendula	A				•	•	•	
Candytuft	A or P					•	•	•
Carnation	A				•	•	•	
Clarkia	A					•	•	•
Coleus	TP	•				•	•	•
Creeping Zinnia	A	•			•	•	•	
Daisies (many types)	P				•	•	•	
Dianthus	A or P					•	•	•
Forget-me-not	B					•	•	•
Fuchsia	TP	•						•
Gazania	A				•	•	•	•
Geranium	TP	•	•		•	•	•	
Impatiens	TP	•			•		•	•
Lantana	TP					•	•	•
Lobelia	A					•	•	•

FLOWER

A—ANNUAL
B—BIENNIAL
P—PERENNIAL[1]
TP—TENDER PERENNIAL[2]

Flower	Type	Hanging Basket	Tub or 2 to 5 Gallon Container	Large Container 8-12 Inch Pot	Small Container 4-6 Inch Pot	Full Sun	Partial Shade	Full Shade
Marigold	A			•	•	•	•	
Mignonette	A				•	•	•	
Morning Glory	A	•				•	•	
Nasturtium	A	•				•	•	
Nemesia	A				•	•	•	
Nemophila	A					•	•	•
Nicotiana	A				•	•	•	
Nierembergia	TP		•	•		•	•	
Pansy	A or P	•				•	•	•
Petunia	A	•				•	•	•
Phlox	A or P				•	•	•	
Portulaca	A	•				•	•	
Primrose	P			•	•		•	•
Salvia	A				•	•	•	
Schizanthus	A		•	•		•	•	
Snapdragon	A				•	•	•	
Sweet Pea	A	•				•	•	
Thunbergia	A	•				•	•	
Vinca	A	•				•	•	
Zinnia	A		•	•		•	•	

1. Perennials, when grown in containers, need protective covering during the Minnesota winter.
2. In Minnesota, tender perennials must either be grown as annuals or brought indoors (usually into a cool, 30-50°F environment) for the winter.

This listing is courtesy of The National Garden Bureau.

Successful Tree Planting

John Ball

Some homeowners believe that planting a tree is the easiest task in the world; just find a spot, dig a hole, and you're done! Nothing could be further from the truth. How carefully a tree is planted will set the stage for how it will grow in the years to come. Since a tree may live for many decades, isn't it worth a little extra effort to start the tree out right?

Buying the Tree

The planting process starts not with planting the tree, but with buying it. Starting with a healthy specimen can insure that your planting care will not be wasted. While at the garden center or nursery, look for trees with the following characteristics: normal shoot growth, no insect or disease problems, and no scars or torn bark. Also note whether the garden center is storing the tree properly.

Regardless of which type of stock is purchased, whether bare root or balled and burlapped (B&B), the same storage care should be continued once the tree is home. Bare-root stock should have roots kept moist in a pail of damp chips or water, and the B&B stock should be kept with the burlap ball covered or hosed down and stored in the shade. If possible, the tree should be planted the day it is purchased. Even better, have the hole dug before you bring the tree home, then plant immediately.

The Planting Hole

Where the hole is dug is very important. In addition to design considerations, homeowners often forget to check three critical items. First, see if the tree has enough room to reach its full height and spread. Always look up before planting, since power lines can cause problems in the years to come. Equally important, yet often neglected, is being certain the tree has enough area for its root system. Mature trees have a root system that extends far beyond the crown. The ground within that area should be free of pavement or other barriers that impede the exchange of oxygen and carbon dioxide between soil and air.

Construction of the planting hole is as critical as its placement.

The hole should be dug no deeper than the depth of the roots, but the width should be several feet wider than the extent of the roots. This area of loose soil will allow more air space.

Fill the planting hole with the same soil you take out. Years ago, nurseries advised backfilling the planting hole with peat moss, composted manure, and rich top soil. This does not benefit the tree, however, and may even be detrimental to its survival. Abrupt changes of texture (soil particle size) has a great effect on moisture flow. If the backfill is coarser (larger particles, such as sand) than the surrounding soil, water may not drain properly.

Some might think that if the soil is poor in their yard, providing a good backfill would help the tree get a good start. If the soil in the yard is that poor, however, perhaps the tree should not be planted; eventually its roots would grow out of the backfill. There are tree species that are native to wet sites, dry sites, and everything in between. Planting a tree that is naturally adapted to the soil in the area would be much wiser than modifying the planting soil to suit the tree.

Planting the Tree

Once the tree is set in the planting hole, be sure it is at the right depth. If it's too high, the roots may dry out; if it's too low, the roots may not receive enough oxygen. For B&B stock, the top of the ball should be at the soil surface. It's better to err in setting it slightly too high than too low, since the weight of the soil ball, especially with large trees, will cause some settling.

For bare-root trees, the depth of planting can be checked by looking at the bud union. Most ornamental trees are grafted, with the above-ground portion of the tree placed on the roots of another plant. At the base of the stem or trunk, there will be a small crook, where the top and roots meet. Place the crook an inch or two above the top of the planting hole.

When placing a bare-root tree in the hole, be sure not to twist any roots. The hole should be deep enough and wide enough to accommodate the roots without bending them. Twisting the roots to fit the hole may result in girdling of the roots as they increase in diameter, eventually resulting in crown die-back as the roots die. Once the roots are properly positioned, place soil around the roots until the hole is one-third filled, then add water. Once the ground has settled, fill another third and repeat the process until the hole is filled. Be sure to complete this entire process as quickly as possible, since the roots that are not covered are prone to drying.

For B&B stock, the same process is followed. Since the root system is enclosed in a burlap ball, there is no need to worry about twisting the roots. The burlap need not be removed; generally it will disintegrate within six months to a year. Plastic wrapping, however, should be carefully cut away and removed; plastic may take years to break down, and during that time, it will restrict root development. Just before the hole is completely filled in, cut away any twine wrapped around the base of the trunk.

Care of the New Tree

With either type of planting material, bare root or B&B, the planting is not finished when the tree is in the ground. Other tasks remain. Be sure to keep a grass-free area (with a radius of at least a foot, more if possible) around the tree. Grass is tough competition for young trees, and they will recover from transplant shock much more quickly if their competition is reduced. This grass-free strip can be left bare, or even better, covered with mulch. A mulch will keep the root area cool and moist. The best mulch is a two or three-inch layer of composted wood chips; a deeper mulch may prevent oxygen from penetrating the soil, while a shallower mulch may not provide any benefit. Composted chips should be used, since fresh chips may have bacteria and draw nitrogen from the soil as they break down.

After planting, a portion of the tree crown is sometimes pruned away, in the belief that since the root area is reduced, the crown must also be reduced. For many species, however, the spring root growth is triggered by the tree's expanding terminal buds, which release a chemical that initiates root growth. If these buds are removed, root growth may be delayed. During the first year after planting, therefore, pruning should be limited to removing broken, diseased, or poorly positioned branches.

There's some question as to whether newly transplanted trees should be fertilized. While most studies have found no harm to fertilizing at transplant time, few have found any benefit. Apparently trees have to recover from transplant shock before fertilizers are useful. This is not true of watering, however. Be sure to water the tree for the first two years after transplanting. New trees can use about one inch of water per week.

If all these steps are followed — proper selection of species and site, carefully constructed planting hole, placement of the tree, and good care after transplanting — the tree will be off to a good start at its new location.

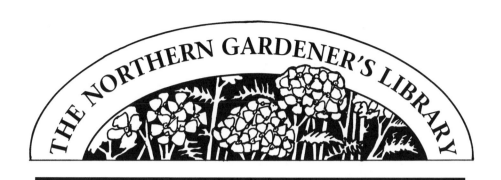

THE NORTHERN GARDENER'S LIBRARY

Chapter 4

Care and Feeding

Maintaining Your Summer Garden

Common-Sense Lawn Care

Reducing Pesticide Use

Putting Your Garden to Bed

Maintaining Your Summer Garden

Fred Glasoe

What do we need to fret about when summer days bless us with lush greenery and lots of color? What if everything in the garden is just as we anticipated it would be when we planted it in the spring? How can we keep the greenery fresh and beautiful and flowers blooming, and how can we be assured of fall production of vegetables and flowers? The secret is a daily summer routine. Regularly scheduled garden tasks are the key to success. Otherwise, the eagerness we feel in April and May is often completely lost by July, and lovely June disintegrates into disastrous August and September.

The basics are simple: first, keep the soil damp with a regular watering schedule; second, prevent weed takeover; third, cut off old flower bloom and keep annual plants pinched back and bushy; fourth, be on the lookout for strange insects or fungus invasion; and fifth, construct a scheduled feeding program.

Water

The overwhelming needs of plants are water, sun, and air with sufficient carbon dioxide. It's not always easy to do something about the latter two, but you can and must be serious about adequate watering. As the days become warmer, much more water is required. Gardeners often underestimate the amount of water plants need. It's really hard on the garden if it is deluged one week and then dried out severely for two or three weeks. Good soil has the characteristic of being able to hold moisture for a long period of time, because it has many tiny air spaces within each square inch. It resembles a sponge, which holds water well, yet has many micro-spaces full of air. The best mixture will include good top soil, sphagnum peat moss, and sharp sand. Generous, heavy watering that does not produce floods of standing water is necessary each week.

Small amounts of water applied every day may never reach an adequate depth, and plants watered in this fashion will form a maze of shallow roots and no enduring deep roots. If the top soil becomes temporarily dry or overheated, these roots will be damaged and the plant will wilt badly. Growth will also be curtailed, and the stunted plant will become a fast-food item for insects and disease. The deeper the root structure, the happier the plant, because its roots can remain cool and moist during the hot summer days.

Weeds

Weeds steal a lot of food and water from our plants. They are gluttons, capable of turning the best garden into the worst. Weed problems are not as difficult to solve as some folks think. We can either spend a great deal of time pulling weeds and scraping the soil, or we can mulch the garden with partially composted leaves, collected each spring and fall.

Pre-emergent herbicides can be used, but it should be kept in mind that they kill the seeds, not the already existent weeds. It should not be necessary to use herbicides year in and year out if there is a good program of soil maintenance, composting, and mulching

Flower maintenance

If you feel overworked and have to struggle in your garden, it just isn't fun. There are easy ways to deal with some of the tedious chores. One of these is cutting off old flowers to promote more bloom and good strong plants. The quiet early morning hours in the morning can be such a pleasant time for tending to this chore. It's nice to pick a few fresh blooms for the breakfast table, or gather a few new vegetables for today's meals.

Pest control

While you enjoy your morning or evening stroll through your garden, be on the lookout for little creatures that hide beneath leaves or in the soft buds of stems and flowers. Mite problems increase on dry, hot days, and aphids get very thirsty for the sweet, wet juices in new growth areas. Fungal diseases work their way through a garden when we are locked into a long rainy spell or when the gardener insists on an evening watering routine and showers the foliage heavily. This water remains on the leaves all night and the fungal spores quickly reproduce and spread over everything that's green and growing.

Roses, mums, phlox, zinnias, and tuberous begonias must be treated early with preventive measures before fungal diseases are allowed to settle in and destroy. Insects that are constant problems, like the cabbage moth, will be made uncomfortable with preventive sprays. You don't want those little yellow beasts laying their eggs on your lovely green leaves. The old adage that an ounce of prevention is worth a pound of cure is still valid in the garden. Whenever possible, non-chemical treatments should be your first course of action. For example, spider mites and aphids are discouraged by a spray of water.

Fertilizing

Fertilizing both vegetables and flowers is important at this time of year. Overfertilizing is just as bad as not feeding at all, and remember that plants, like people, have different dietary preferences. If you want leaves, feed the plants a lot of nitrogen. If it's blooms you want, it might be best to skimp on nitrogen. Stems and roots need potash and phosphorous for strong development. Both of these, especially the phosphorous, will help flowers to form and bloom. Adequate nitrogen improves the quality of your foliage, but if your soil is heavy, keep in mind that a small amount will last a long time. Many new gardeners overfeed their annuals, and a shortage of blooms is evident on oversized, leafy plants.

June and July are good times to fertilize trees and shrubs. Trees, because of their size, finally become too big for a full meal to take hold immediately. Deep-rooted trees have roots that are too far down for practical fertilizing, but trees do need your extra help and care during the first five or ten years they spend in your yard. Shrubs should be fertilized both in early spring and again in midsummer. A balanced 10-10-10 fertilizer benefits all woody plants, but it must be worked into the root area at the drip line and watered into the soil.

By June, perennials are up and growing well. It's possible some are growing too well. This is a good time to divide fibrous root varieties and either replant them in your "need spots" or dump them. Don't save every little thing, and don't save sickly looking plants. This is always a fine time to do a little rearranging and add new species that can be found on sale. If you don't like the plant that never has looked good, get it out and buy what you really enjoy. Thinning out and replacing is a good way to develop more color in the garden.

I know you aren't upside down in the soil all the time, so get out and see other gardens and enjoy your garden friends. Look for public gardens in your town or neighborhood, or sneak a peak at some of the not-so-public ones (with the owner's permission, of course). The only drawback is that you will come home with more ideas and wishes than you can possibly put into operation. Save some time to sit back and enjoy — midsummer, unlike mid-life, doesn't have to be a time of crisis.

Common-Sense Lawn Care

Donald P. Olson

With the drought and heat taking their toll on many lawns in the late 1980s, home owners are now seeking lawn maintenance practices that will lead to healthy, long-lived lawns. A common-sense lawn care approach — where you look at fertilization, mowing, weed control, and watering in relation to how grass grows — will help reduce the time and effort associated with obtaining a high-quality lawn.

In the cool, humid regions of the United States, most lawns consist of Kentucky bluegrass, with many also containing fine fescues and the new turf types of perennial rye grasses. In common-sense lawn care, focus is placed on the development of a strong root system to enhance the overall growth of these three cool-season grasses.

Contrary to many ways of thinking, most of the maintenance associated with a high-quality lawn should be done in the fall. Preparing lawns for the winter is directed toward creating conditions for optimum vigor and growth the following season. Helping lawns develop strong roots in the fall also gives them maximum protection against winter snows and ice. Encouraging a healthy plant and strong root system in the fall will result in a beautiful, low-maintenance lawn the following year.

Fertilization

Proper fertilization has an effect on both the present and future health of a lawn. Excessive use of fertilizer, especially nitrogen, can promote disease and lead to excessive top growth and thatch buildup. A common-sense fertilizer program provides for uniform growth throughout the season.

The three nutrients primarily needed for grass growth are nitrogen, phosphorus (phosphoric acid), and potassium (potash), with nitrogen usually being required in the largest amounts. Nitrogen is responsible for dark green color, leaf development, and improving the density of the lawn and root system. Since grass plants use large amounts of nitrogen, it needs to be replaced regularly. In most lawn fertilizers, nitrogen (the first of the three numbers on a fertilizer bag)

79

makes up the largest component of the mixture.

The amount of nitrogen used each year dictates the level of maintenance a lawn will require. If you enjoy golfing or boating on week-ends, you will probably want to use lower rates of nitrogen. If what you are after is a very high-quality lawn, then more nitrogen is required, along with more maintenance.

Because a grass plant uses nitrogen to produce carbohydrates that are stored in the fall when the plant is preparing for winter dormancy, the majority of the nitrogen should be applied in the fall. The buildup of carbohydrates enables plants to withstand environmental stresses. Too much nitrogen in the spring leads to excessive vegetative growth and rapid depletion of carbohydrates.

A rule of thumb is to apply one-third of the total nitrogen in spring and two-thirds in the fall. If you are applying three pounds of nitrogen per 1,000 square feet per year, you should apply one pound in late May, one pound in September, and one pound in early to mid-October.

Phosphorus and potash play minor roles in an established lawn but are still important and may be lacking in some soils. Soil should be tested to determine if it is low in either of these nutrients. Soil test information is available at your local county extension office.

Mowing

Like it or not, mowing is a maintenance ritual that must be performed regularly. When done properly, mowing contributes greatly to the overall health and quality of a lawn.

A grass plant's root system grows in proportion to the height of the plant. The higher the setting on your mower, the deeper the root system. Remember, a deeper root system is able to reach water and other nutrients buried at greater depth in the soil. This explains why many lawns mowed at less than 1-1/2 inches during a dry summer don't survive the drought and heat stress.

Mowing height should follow the growth rate of the plant. Start out low in the spring, higher in the summer, and then low again in the fall. With cool-season grasses, best results are obtained by mowing at 1-1/2 to 2 inches in spring and fall, and 3 inches in mid-summer. Avoid cutting more than one-third of the grass blade in any one mowing. This results in stress to the plant and root loss.

Another common-sense tip is to mow in a different direction each week. A lawn looks good not because the grass has been cut short, but because the grass has a uniform height. Mowing a different direction prevents the blades from leaning to one side, causing the mower to leave skips and uneven areas.

Grass Clippings

In most cases there is no need to worry about grass clippings. If you mow regularly and the clippings never get too long, simply allow them to remain on the lawn. They will decompose and return nutrients, especially nitrogen, back to the soil. Over the course of a growing season, clippings return about one pound of nitrogen per 1,000 square feet. That amounts to $10 to $15 worth of lawn fertilizer each year.

Home owners have a number of options for disposing of their grass clippings — including composting themselves, using as mulch, or taking them to a compost site — but leaving them on the lawn is the most cost effective and environmentally sound way to handle grass clippings.

Thatch Control

Thatch, the brown layer of the lawn found between the soil surface and the green vegetation is made up of living and dead stems and roots. It occurs when roots and stems build up, exceeding the rate of decay.

Thatch is only a problem when it becomes 1/2-inch thick or more. Excess thatch harbors diseases and prevents nutrients, water, and air from getting into the soil. Over time, the root system begins to grow only into the thatch layer, unable to penetrate the soil, resulting in a very shallow root system. When we have a stressful year, lawns with heavy thatch buildup and shallow root systems will die.

The best time to deal with thatch is early spring or early fall. Core aerification is preferred over the use of a de-thatching machine or power rake. A power rake lifts the dead grass, blades, and stems to the surface but doesn't penetrate the deeper thatch layer. Aerification involves the use of a machine that punches a hollow tine into the soil and removes a core of soil and thatch. Coring a lawn permits better infiltration of water and fertilizer. Make sure to only use an aerifier that actually lifts the soil out of the ground and not the type that simply punches holes in the soil. An aerifying machine should be used in several different directions to provide a good pattern of cores, thus providing a better environment for soil microorganisms to work and actively decompose the components of thatch.

Because thatch buildup is greater on high-maintenance lawns, annual core aerification is a must for those lawns that are receiving four to five pounds of nitrogen per 1,000 square feet per year.

Weed Control

Control of broad-leaf weeds in lawns is easier and more effective in the fall than any other time of the year. There is less chance of herbicides damaging trees and shrubs in late August and September, and controlling broad-leaf weeds in the fall gets you off to a weed-free spring.

Dandelions are a good example. These pervasive weeds are biennials, which means they germinate one year and flower the next. A September application of a broad-leaf weed killer kills all the dandelions present, including those which germinated over the course of the summer and will flower and produce seed next spring. This is the most effective way to stop the cycle from continuing.

The cheapest form of weed control is grass competition. Common-sense management practices increase the ability of desirable lawn grasses to compete for nutrients, space, light, and moisture. A strong lawn will limit the invasion of new weeds and tend to crowd out existing weeds. Again, maintaining good soil conditions, proper fertilization, careful watering, and proper mowing will insure a competitive grass plant.

Watering

The secret to watering is to water deep and less frequently. Your lawn can survive an occasional drying out and may actually benefit from the stress a dry period causes to moisture-loving weeds and fungi.

A lawn needs about one inch of water per week in the summer. This is especially important if you are on a high-maintenance program. To get an indication of the rate of water your sprinkler delivers, place some shallow cans in the spray pattern and measure the water in the can that has been applied over an hour.

Municipal water pressure from which our sprinklers operate will generally produce three-quarters inch of water per hour of operation. If you plan to maintain a green lawn all summer, this means that in order to obtain one inch of water per week the sprinkler will have to run four hours on one location. Light watering of the lawn and garden will cause the roots to move upward to where the moisture is located. When moisture is no longer available, the roots are subject to moisture stress. Deep watering fosters deep roots.

Maintaining a good lawn may seem an impossible task to many. However, when correct information and procedures are used, the goal of green grass is easily obtained. The secret is in knowing when the grass is green enough.

Reducing Pesticide Use

Katharine D. Widin

Most gardeners want to reduce their reliance on chemicals to control insects and diseases in their yards and gardens. Here are a few tips to help you in that direction.

Start with Healthy Plants

Don't be tempted by the forlorn, scraggly, yellow, half-priced rejects at local discount stores. Most plants which look sick are sick. Overgrown, crowded plants that have received cursory care often harbor insects and diseases. Pass these by and choose sturdy, well-tended plants with good color. If you are buying woody plants, check the stems carefully for wounds, dry or oozing cankers, and insect or egg masses. Check leaves for feeding insects, fungal leaf spots and the crinkly, mottled look of viral infections.

To keep your plants healthy, plant them in recommended growing locations, and provide them with the amount of fertilizer and water appropriate for the species. Organic mulches and amendments which improve the soil will also encourage good plant growth.

Resistant Varieties

When possible, grow varieties that are resistant to pests. If you insist on having that beautiful, flowering crab apple that is very susceptible to apple scab, you may have no alternative but to spray fungicides on it throughout the growing season. When purchasing new plants, investigate their resistance to common insect and disease problems. Consider mildew-resistant zinnias, wilt-resistant tomatoes, aphid-resistant honeysuckle, blackknot-resistant *Prunus*, and pest-resistant shrub roses. If you have existing plantings that include a variety that is highly susceptible to a particular problem, educate yourself as to the best materials and timing for control.

Proper Identification and Control

Knowing the identity of the insect or disease which is attacking the plant, the recommended control, and the proper timing of implementation are among the most important aspects of effectively controlling a problem. Many chemicals are needlessly sprayed by well-meaning individuals who cannot identify the correct symptoms, causes, and treatments.

For example, dry, papery leaves which appear on birch trees in June are usually caused by the birch leaf miner, a sawfly which lays its eggs on birch leaves in May. One spray with Orthene in May when leaf miners are small will control the problem, whereas spraying the tree once the leaves are dry and papery has no effect.

When using pesticides, apply no more than the label rate and mix only what you need. Buy small packages if you use the pesticide in small amounts or infrequently.

Rotation and Sanitation

To reduce pest problems in your yard and garden, crop rotation and good garden cleanup are good habits to form.

Rotation is the practice of moving annual plants every year or two to a different area of your garden. Many insect and disease agents can build up in the soil over time and eventually cause serious infestations or disease outbreaks.

For example, tomatoes should be moved to a different area of the garden each year. Relatives of tomatoes such as peppers, potatoes, and eggplants should not be planted in areas where tomatoes were recently grown either.

Instead, plant an unrelated plant, such as peas, on an old tomato plot, since they will not be susceptible to most insects and diseases which affect tomatoes.

Sanitation is the practice of ridding the growing area of dead, diseased, or insect-infested plant material that could serve as a source of infection to healthy plants. Pruning old raspberry canes not only makes way for new ones, but also removes borers and some leaf-spot and canker fungi from the raspberry bed. Removing old asparagus fronds, ridding shrubs and trees of dead wood, removing plant debris from the garden in the fall, are all forms of sanitation.

Organic Controls

For many insect and disease problems there are effective controls that do not involve the use of synthetic pesticides. Biological controls, such as *Bacillus thuringienses* (Dipel), a bacterium specific for moth and butterfly larvae, are effective and safe for humans and the environment. Botanical insecticides, such as rotenone and pyrethrum, and insecticidal soaps are pesticides which degrade fairly rapidly under environmental conditions, yet are very effective at controlling insects.

The fruit damage caused by the apple maggot can be controlled satisfactorily by hanging sticky decoy apples in host trees. Laying a piece of tar paper on the soil surrounding the stems of cabbage transplants to protect them from cabbage maggot larvae, and putting collars around the stems of tomatoes as cutworm deterrents are effective barrier methods of control. Tilling soil exposes overwintering larvae and fungal spores to drying and natural predators.

You can have a healthy garden using fewer pesticides. Healthy, hardy plant material, good plant culture and care, knowledge of pests and diseases and their control, using rotation and sanitation and other effective alternative control measures are all steps in the right direction — steps that will lead to abundant harvests and colorful flower beds, along with a healthier and safer environment.

Gardening Skill

The safe use of pesticides should be a concern of every home gardener. Safety involves a combination of knowledge, common sense, and the ability to follow directions. Any misuse of pesticides could result in poisoning of the gardener, family members, neighbors, pets, or consumers of the produce.

There are many practices which a home gardener can follow to reduce the need for pesticides. Here are some of them:

- Locate the garden on well-drained soil, away from shade, where there is good air movement.

- Keep garden and surrounding area free of weeds and old plant material that might harbor insects and disease.

- Develop a 3-4 year rotation for the garden so that the same area does not have the same plants year after year.

- When available, purchase plant or vegetable varieties which are resistant to disease, nematodes, and insects.

- Use mechanical means of pest control; that is, cultivate to control weeds, pick off insects, and destroy diseased plants.

- Use biological controls when available, for example, *Bacillus thuringienis* for moth and butterfly larvae.

Putting Your Garden to Bed

Fred Glasoe

As autumn approaches, we gardeners never know whether we will have an early freeze or the blessing of a late fall garden. But one thing we do know for sure is that the end is very near. The pleasures of the summer garden come to a halt, and we are propelled into planning for next year's planting adventure. This is truly the best time to assess garden gains and losses and create the design for the season to come.

Winter Mulch. The trash bags stacked along the alleys in piles awaiting garbage pickup have the potential for a higher destiny. They can be put to use in your garden as good protective cover for your perennials and roses. You can use the three-ply plastic bags of leaves just as they are, piling them on your flower beds. They can be removed when winter is over and stored behind your garage until mid-June, when they can be used as a fine summer mulch. By fall this mulch will be well broken down and can be worked into the soil as a soil amendment.

If your area is deficient in oak, maple, or linden leaves, drive to the nearest oak forest. You will probably be welcomed if you offer to haul leaves. In a short time you can present your garden at home with a nice insulating blanket.

Planting Bulbs. Remember last July when you were so taken by the blazing lily display in the other fellow's garden? October is bulb planting month, especially for lilies and tulips. Many growers have dug and divided their bulbs by now and will be having fall sales in early October. Don't buy a bulb planter unless your soil is very loose and light. My soil is too heavy and I find a moist glob of soil gets stuck in the planting tube. It's easier to dig a trench or a large oval. This also has the advantage of making it possible to set the bulbs in a nice pattern. I stir a little bone meal into the softened soil at the bottom of the trench. The trench covers up quickly and is well tucked in for the winter.

Avoid trying to grow lilies if your soil is extremely heavy. If you are determined in spite of this word of caution, work in a large amount of sharp sand, peat moss, and compost before you plant. Good drainage is the key to both gorgeous tulips and beautiful lilies.

Dahlias. Tuberous roots and tubers need to be dug in the late fall if you plan to use them again next year. Dahlias and cannas can be left in the ground two or three weeks after the first killing frost. This aids them in becoming dormant for winter storage. Dahlias seem to do better in winter storage if they remain frost free for a lengthy growing time in the fall. A gradual cooling down in fall helps all of our hardy plants make it through the cold northern winter in better condition.

Tubers should be stored in an area which can be maintained at 40°-50°F. They must be carefully monitored for excessive moisture, which can lead to rot, and also for extreme dryness, which can cause them to shrivel up to nothing. I have tried every type of cleaning, drying, spraying, dipping, and storage media for my dahlias. In retrospect, I have had the best luck when I have allowed the soil to remain on the roots. I spread them out along the coldest wall in the darkest, coolest corner of my unheated basement storage room.

Dahlias usually come through the winter in good condition if they can be dug late and if the storage area stays cool. If you store gladiolus corms or begonia tubers, it is best to dust them well with a pesticide made expressly for this purpose. Most garden stores stock this product.

Geraniums. If we haven't experienced a hard frost by October, it's fun to save some of those lovely and expensive geraniums from the summer garden. I was never too impressed with the semi-dried plants that were hung up in Grandma's basement for the winter. They were replanted in May and looked awful until August.

A better way to overwinter geraniums is to take small cuttings and grow them under fluorescent lights. They grow wonderfully and you can make additional cuttings from them by midwinter. Eighteen hours of timed lighting in a cool basement will enable you to start your next year's geraniums before you have this year's garden put to bed.

As Old Man Winter trudges toward us, get ready to enjoy your indoor garden and next spring's seedlings. Prepare your November list and include reminders for clean pots and fresh bags of potting soil, vermiculite, sphagnum moss, and water-soluble fertilizer.

Your Fall Lawn and Garden Checklist

September

☐ Read all pesticide labels before purchasing and applying.

☐ Plant potted hardy chrysanthemums for instant fall color and bloom next year.

☐ Harvest squash, gourds, melons and pumpkins before frost; store only if fully ripe.

☐ Properly cure and store garden vegetables to prevent rotting.

☐ Apply first of two lawn fertilizations; fall is the best time to fertilize your lawn.

☐ Seed lawns the first half of the month.

☐ Lay sod.

☐ Aerate lawns to relieve compaction and reduce thatch build-up.

☐ Remove and destroy mushrooms appearing in lawns.

☐ Spray for broadleaf weeds if you have not just seeded the lawn. September is the most effective time to control weeds like dandelions and creeping charlie.

☐ Plant evergreens; continue to water young trees and shrubs every 10 to 14 days if weather is dry.

☐ Start a compost pile for fall leaves and garden debris.

☐ Caulk and seal cracks or other openings insects may use to enter homes.

☐ Apply an 18-inch band of diazinon or chlorpyrifos around the foundation if sowbugs and millipedes invade homes.

☐ Don't attempt to control wasps now. Control efforts around the house can drive them indoors; wasp activity will stop soon.

☐ Check cupboards for flour beetles and other pantry insects. Discard or sterilize infested products.

☐ Bring in houseplants, hibiscus, Christmas cactus and amaryllis bulbs which summered outdoors. Check for insects and wash thoroughly.

☐ Cap chimneys with wire mesh to prevent squirrels or raccoons from entering or nesting in chimneys in spring. If a chimney is already capped, check that it is secure.

☐ If moles and gophers were a yard problem this summer, September-October is a good time to trap them. Mortality in the fall will reduce breeding populations in spring.

October

☐ Wrap young and thin-barked trees with tree wrap to prevent sunscald.

☐ Protect young trees with rabbit and rodent guards.

- ☐ Plant spring-flowering bulbs outdoors or force several in containers for indoor bloom in February.
- ☐ Plant garden lily bulbs for bloom next summer.
- ☐ Apply second application of lawn fertilizer in late October.
- ☐ Rake leaves off lawns to minimize snowmold damage.
- ☐ Continue to mow lawns until growth stops. Don't catch clippings.
- ☐ Protect roses and mulch perennials and bulb beds.
- ☐ Prune large shade trees.
- ☐ If bats were inside during summer, seal up existing entryways and holes to prevent their return next year. Check to make sure no bats are inside before sealing openings
- ☐ If you feed birds, place feeders away from buildings; bird feed may attract small animals which may find their way into buildings. Store bird food securely to exclude mice and squirrels.
- ☐ Don't feed birds if you have problems with woodpeckers. Woodpeckers may be more likely to frequent areas where other birds feed.
- ☐ Clean out and repair bird houses so they will be ready for use in the spring.
- ☐ Consider building bird houses, nest boxes and other structures for wildlife so they are ready in early spring when the animals will be looking for denning and nesting sites. Remove roofs or leave clean-outs open to discourage rodent use.
- ☐ Remove bird nests from buildings or other structures where they are a problem Use nylon bird netting to prevent birds returning in spring.
- ☐ Mark fireblight cankers for removal in late winter.

November

- ☐ Remove garden debris (debris allows diseases and insects to survive the winter).
- ☐ Clean and oil garden tools before storing for winter.
- ☐ Caulk and plug any entrances in and around the home which wasps used this past season.
- ☐ Buy new African violets to brighten the inside of your house.
- ☐ Reduce houseplant fertilization and watering as days shorten and growth slows.
- ☐ Send Thanksgiving flowers to a friend. Potted mums last for weeks.
- ☐ Plant amaryllis for giant Christmas blooms.
- ☐ Make first application of repellent spray to shrubs and young trees for protection from deer damage.

Source: U of M Extension Service

THE NORTHERN GARDENER'S LIBRARY

Chapter 5

Appendices

Mail Order Sources

Zone Hardiness Map

About the Authors

Mail Order Sources

NAME OF COMPANY	TYPE OF MERCHANDISE	REMARKS
Stokes Seeds, Inc. Box 548 Buffalo, NY 14240	All kinds of seeds; good selection	Good all around source, excellent cultural advice, excellent source of vegetable seeds
Park Seed Co. Cokesbury Rd. Greenwood, SC 29647	All kinds of seeds, good selection, unusual garden perennials	Good all around source, excellent cultural advice, house plant seeds
Harris Seeds 961 Lyell Ave. Rochester, NY 14606	All kinds of seeds	Very reliable, good source for vegetables
Thompson & Morgan P.O. Box 1308 Jackson, NJ 08527	All kinds of seeds	Good source with an English flare
Farmer Seed & Nursery Faribault, MN 55021	All kinds of seeds & nursery stock	Local source, very reliable
Antonelli Brothers 2545 Capitola Rd. Santa Cruz, CA 95062	Tuberous begonia seed, tuberous begonias & gloxinia	Very reliable
Gardener's Supply 128 Intervale Rd. Burlington, VT 05401	Innovative garden equipment & gadgets	Very reliable
Van Ness Water Gardens 2460 N. Euclid Ave. Upland, CA 91786	Water lilies, bog plants, pond equipment	Excellent catalog
Burpee & Co. Warminister, PA 18974	Seeds, bulbs, plants, nursery stock	Very reliable
Heritage Gardens 1 Meadow Ridge Rd., Shenandoah, IA 51601	Garden perennials, vines, fruit trees, shrubs, shade trees	Reliable local source
Busse Gardens Rt. 2, Box 238 Cokato, MN 55321	Good variety of garden perennials	Good local source for all perennials
Ambergate Gardens 8015 Krey Ave. Waconia, MN 55387	Unusual garden perennials, Martagon lilies	Good local source for garden perennials
Borbeleta Gardens 15974 Canby Ave. Faribault, MN 55021	Daylilies, lilies, irises daffodils, Siberian irises	Good local source with excellent catalog

NAME OF COMPANY	TYPE OF MERCHANDISE	REMARKS
Van Bourgondien P.O. Box A 245 Farmindale Rd., Rt. 109 Babylon, NY 11702	Seasonal bulbs	Good source
Epicure Seeds Ltd. P.O. Box 450 Brewster, NY 10509	Unusual vegetables	European flare
Johnny's Selected Seeds Albion, ME 04910	Vegetable specialist	Good catalog with excellent cultural instructions
L. L. Olds Seed Co. P.O. Box 7790 2901 Packers Ave. Madison, WI 53707-7790	All seeds plus nursery stock	Good local source
Vermont Bean Seed Co. Garden Lane, Bomoseen VT 05732	Vegetable specialist	Good source, very unusual
Gurney's Seed & Nursery Co. 110 Capital St. Yankton, SD 57079	All kinds of seeds & nursery stock	Good source
Earl May Seed & Nursery Shenandoah, IA 51603	Seed & nursery stock	Good local source
Jung Seed Co. Randolph, WI 53956	Seeds, house plants, garden perennials	Good local source
North Star Gardens 19060 Manning Tr. Marine, MN 55047	Raspberry & blueberry specialist	Aimed at the market grower, good catalog
Jordan Seeds 6400 Upper Afton Rd. Woodbury, MN 55125	Vegetable seeds, market growers supplies	Aimed at the market gardener
Wilson Bros, Floral Co. Roachdale, IN 46172	Geranium specialist, African violets, fuchsia, begonias, house plants	Very reliable, good source
Donahue's Gardens P.O. Box366 420 S. W. 10th St. Faribault, MN 55021	Minnesota garden chrysanthemums, clematis, begonias, assorted hanging material	Excellent source for garden mums, local source with good quality
Prairie Restorations, Inc. P.O. Box 327 Princeton, MN 55371	Seeds for MN native prairie grasses & wild flowers	MN genotypes, locally grown

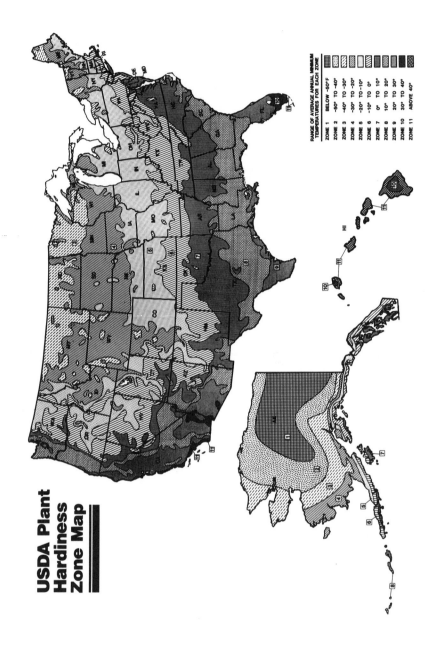

USDA Plant Hardiness Zone Map

RANGE OF AVERAGE ANNUAL MINIMUM TEMPERATURES FOR EACH ZONE
ZONE 1   BELOW -50°F
ZONE 2   -50° TO -40°
ZONE 3   -40° TO -30°
ZONE 4   -30° TO -20°
ZONE 5   -20° TO -10°
ZONE 6   -10° TO 0°
ZONE 7   0° TO 10°
ZONE 8   10° TO 20°
ZONE 9   20° TO 30°
ZONE 10 30° TO 40°
ZONE 11 ABOVE 40°

About the Authors

John Ball has a PhD in Urban Forestry and currently works in the commercial tree service industry. Before moving to Duluth, Minnesota, John taught horticulture in Michigan and Minnesota.

Lina Belar grows herbs and other good things to eat in Perham, Minnesota, and has been a commercial producer of culinary herbs.

Deborah Brown, St. Paul, coordinates horticultural resources to answer questions from the public as director for the U of M Extension Service Dial-U Clinic. She also speaks and writes about gardening in Minnesota.

Jon Bryan Burley is assistant professor of landscape architecture at Colorado State University, Fort Collins, Colorado.

Mary Bydlon is a member of the Minnesota Herb Society who wrote a long-running column in *Minnesota Horticulturist* on cooking with herbs. She lives in Edina, Minnesota.

Fred Glasoe, Minneapolis, Minnesota, is a regular contributor to *Minnesota Horticulturist*, as well as the host of a weekly radio program on gardening. An avid promoter of gardening in the North, Fred is past president of MSHS and a life member of the organization.

Dick Gray wrote a column for *Minnesota Horticulturist* entitled "Beyond the Garden" during the 1980s. He is the founder of the Freshwater Biological Institute, a nationwide environmental organization.

Margaret Haapoja gardens and writes about horticulture for Zone 3 from Bovey, Minnesota.

Kate Hintz is an avid gardener who planted her new garden during 1988 in Mahtomedi, Minnesota.

Beth Jarvis tries new gardening methods in Crystal, Minnesota. Her background is in journalism, and she is working on a degree in horticulture.

Dorothy Johnson is Executive Director of MSHS. She has been a Master Gardener in Dakota County since 1977, and is active in local and regional garden organizations.

Robert E. Kelly, Minneapolis, Minnesota, is a member of the Men's Garden Club of Minneapolis and the Dahlia Society.

Emely Lincowski, formerly from Chisago County, Minnesota, is now a landscape designer in Pleasanton, California.

Donald Olson is employed by the U of M Extension Service, and formerly served as horticultural agent with Ramsey County, Minnesota.

Reverend Lawrence Rule began gardening in Southern Minnesota and, now that he's retired, tests All-American Selections for Zone 3 at his garden in Brainerd, Minnesota.

Katharine Widin is a plant pathologist, who is employed as a City Forester as well as maintaining a horticultural consulting firm in Stillwater, Minnesota.